IRISH EMIGRANTS IN NORTH AMERICA

Part Nine

By David Dobson

CLEARFIELD

Copyright © 2018
by David Dobson
All Rights Reserved

ISBN 9780806358727

INTRODUCTION

Irish emigration to North America can be said to have commenced in earnest in the early eighteenth century with the 'Scots-Irish' in 1718. There had been some Irish settlement among the English colonies along the Atlantic coast, some involuntary, in the late seventeenth century; however, much more significant numbers of Irish people could already be found in the English colonies in the West Indies, and to a limited degree, in the Dutch colonies there. For example, the island of Montserrat was almost entirely an Irish settlement. Oliver Cromwell dispatched shiploads of Irish prisoners of war to the Caribbean. Some of them and their descendants are believed to have made their way north to the mainland colonies in due course. There was significant trade between Ireland and the West Indies during the seventeenth and eighteenth centuries which would have led to settlement there, especially by indentured servants or by felons banished to the colonies. Some Irish men and women also emigrated to America and the West Indies via English ports such as Bristol, Liverpool and London. By the eighteenth century, the Irish comprised the largest group of immigrants from the Britain to settle in the Thirteen Colonies.

This volume is based on information from sources concerning individuals who vacated Ireland for the promise of the New World between roughly 1670 and 1830, primary located in Ireland, the United States, Canada, Scotland, and the West Indies. Sources include manuscripts, newspapers and journals, monumental inscriptions, and government records. For each person identified by Dr. Dobson we are given the full name, whereabouts, a date, and the source. In many cases, the entries also provide the ship travelled on, occupation, name(s) of parents and/or spouse, where buried, etc. As with some of the other volumes in this series, researchers will discover a number of emigrants who left Ireland prior to 1775.

David Dobson, Dundee, Scotland, 2018.

IRISH EMIGRANTS IN NORTH AMERICA, Volume 9

REFERENCES

AJ	=	Aberdeen Journal
BNL	=	Belfast News Letter
CA	=	Cork Archives
CLRO	=	City London Record Office
CM	=	Caledonian Mercury, series
CSPI	=	Cal. State Papers, Ireland
DRD	=	Dublin Register of Deeds
FDJ	=	Freeman's Dublin Journal,
FLJ	=	Finn's Leinster Journal
FMC	=	Flynn's Hibernian Chronicle,
GM	=	Gentleman's Magazine
HMC	=	Historical Manuscripts Commission
JCTP	=	Journal of the Council for Trade and the Plantations
LJ	=	Londonderry Journal
LRO	=	London Record Office
MI	=	Monumental Inscription
NARA	=	National Archives, Records
NRS	=	National Records Scotland
NEHGR	=	New England Historic Genealogical Register

NLI =	National Library Ireland
PaGaz	Pennsylvania Gazette
PaJl =	Pennsylvania Journal
PANB =	Public Archives, New Brunswick
PROI =	Public Record Office, Ireland
PRONI =	Public Record Office, Northern Ireland
PWI =	Prerogative Wills of Ireland
StAUR =	St Andrews University Register, 1747-1897
SPG	Society for Propagation of the Gospels
TNA =	The National Archives, Kew
UJA =	Ulster Journal Archaeology
WHM =	Walker's Hibernian Magazine

IRISH EMIGRANTS IN NORTH AMERICA, Volume 9

ABBOT, SAMUEL, a merchant in Philadelphia, Pennsylvania, will, 1789. [PWI]

ACHMUTY, ROBERT, President of the Irish Charitable Society of Boston in 1740. [UJA.II.1.18]

ADAMS, Sergeant JAMES, in Montserrat in 1677-1678. [TNA]

ADAMS, JOHN S., born 1780, a merchant from County Antrim, was naturalised in South Carolina on 21 April 1804. [NARA.M1183/1]

ADDISON, NICHOLAS, Captain of the 52nd Regiment in Boston, will, 1776. [PWI]

ALDERCHURCH, EDWARD, a founder member of the Irish Charitable Society of Boston in 1736. [UJA.II.1.18]

ALEXANDER, GEORGE, born 1772, a ship carpenter from Londonderry, was naturalised in South Carolina on 25 May 1805. [NARA.M1183/1]

ALLEN, ALEXANDER, a merchant in Kingston, Jamaica, will, 1784. [PWI]

ALLEN, GEORGE, in Kingston, Upper Canada, letters, 1842. [PRONI.D4031.F19.1]

ALLEN, JOHN, died in Pennsylvania in 1733.
[Lancaster County Historical Society, inventories, box 1, folder 1]

ALLEN, TIMOTHY, in Richmond, Virginia, will, 1785. [PWI]

AMORY, ROBERT, a planter in Antigua, will, 1713. [PWI]

ANDREWS, JOHN, with a woman, in Montserrat in 1677-1678. [TNA]

ANNESLEY, JAMES, born 1726 in Dunmaine, County Wexford, was kidnapped in Dublin and sold in Delaware as an indentured servant, in 1740 he absconded to Philadelphia and took passage to Kingston, Jamaica, where he enrolled in the Royal Navy. After being discharged in 1741 he returned to the British Isles and eventually to Dublin where he took court action to obtain his birth-rights. James died 5 January 1760.

ANNESLEY, WILLIAM GROVE, a Captain of the 4th Regiment, fourth son of General A. G. Annesley in County Cork, married Elia Taylor, second daughter of John Taylor of Good Hope Estate, Jamaica, in St Michael's, Port Royal Mountains, Jamaica, on 8 March 1866. [GM.ns3/1.737]

ANTHONY, JOSEPH, a physician from County Tyrone, was naturalised in South Carolina on 22 May 1798. [NARA.M1183/1]

ARABIN, FREDERICK, a Captain of the Royal Artillery, son of H Arabin in Maglove, County Meath, married Eliza Mountain, daughter of the Bishop of Quebec, there on 3 May 1823. [GM.93.367]

ARCHDEACON, KATHERINE, born 1685, a spinster from Bramhall Town in County Kilkenny, emigrated via Liverpool to America in 1704. [LRO]

ARMSTRONG, JANE, daughter of Margaret Armstrong [1797-1853], of Castlewellan, County Down, wife of .....Shannon, settled in New Orleans, Louisiana. [Shankhill gravestone, Belfast]

ARMSTRONG, WILLIAM, emigrated aboard the Needham, Captain Cheevers, bound for Newcastle, Delaware, in 1773. [PaJl:8.9.1773]

AUSTIN, WILLIAM, born 1780 in County Tyrone, a merchant who was naturalised in South Carolina on 2 October 1805. [NARA.M1183/1]

BABINGTON, LUCAS, from Newry, brother-in-law of R. Lawrenson of Mount Drummond, and son-in-law of Charles Pasley in Dublin, died in St Louis, Missouri, in 1851. [GM.ns36.216]

BADHAM, ARTHUR B., formerly of Trinity College, Dublin, died on passage to the West Indies on 4 February 1836. [GM.ns5.567]

BAGET, ELIZABETH, youngest daughter of Colonel Baget in Burney, County Kildare, and wife of Colonel Edward K. S. Butler, died in Nova Scotia on 4 November 1846. [GM.ns27.111]

BAGGE, Reverend John, in the parish of St Ann, County of Essex, Virginia, will, 1726. [PWI]

BAGOTT, CHARLES HERBERT, a Lieutenant of the 32nd Regiment of Foot, Engineer of St Vincent, British West Indies, died there in 1765. [FDJ.4004]

BAINES, TORRENCE, in Montserrat in 1677-1678. [TNA]

BAKER, SAMUEL, in Hallowell, Upper Canada, a letter, 1823. [PROI.15c.33]

BARBER, CHARLES, from Kilkenny, an indentured servant aboard the Eleanor of Ireland, master Nicholas Reynolds, bound for Virginia in 1698. [LRO]

BARLOR, CHARITY, from Kilkenny, an indentured servant bound from Liverpool to America in 1698. [LRO]

BARRY, GARRETT, of Montserrat, died in Cornwall, probate, 1659, PCC. [TNA]

BARRY, EDMOND, in the parish of Sandy Point, St Kitts on 7 February 1678. [TNA.COI.42]

BARRY, GARRETT, in the parish of Sandy Point, St Kitts on 7 February 1678. [TNA.COI.42]

BARRY, JAMES, in St Kitts, probate, 1659, PCC. [TNA]

BARRY, JAMES, in Montserrat in 1677-1678. [TNA]

BARRY, Reverend JAMES, born 1708 in County Kildare, educated at the University of Dublin, Rector of St George's parish in Antigua for nine years, died 11 December 1747, husband of Margaret Sherwood. [St John's Cathedral, Antigua]

BARRY, JOHN, from Cork, an indentured servant bound from Bristol to Virginia in 1659. [BRO]

BARRY, Lieutenant RICHARD, in Montserrat in 1677-1678. [TNA]

BARRY, ROBERT, in Montserrat in 1677-1678. [TNA]

BARRY, ROBERT, a merchant in Jamaica, later in Cork, will, 1733. [PWI]

BARRY, WILLIAM, in Montserrat in 1677-1678. [TNA]

BASLEY, WILLIAM, born 1752 in Ireland, via London aboard the Pennsylvania Packet bound for Philadephia in 1775. [TNA.T47.9/11]

BATTEN, JOHN, in Montserrat in 1677-1678. [TNA]

BEATTY, JAMES, son of James Beatty of Dromore died in 1829 and his wife Mary Beatty who died in 1878, settled in USA by 1899. [Dromore Cathedral gravestone]

BELL, JOHN, a weaver in Antrim, who entered the 58th Regiment in northern Ireland in 1757, served at the Siege of Louisbourg in 1758, from there to Halifax, Nova Scotia, fought on the Plains of Abraham, in Canada for three years, via New York to Havannah but captured by a French man-o-war and taken to France, released and rejoined the 58th in Ireland, in 1768 he volunteered for the 65th Regiment bound for Boston, from there to Halifax, served there for six years before being discharged, then he was a watchman at the dock-yard, briefly settled in Shelburne, and thereafter worked in the Royal Engineers in Halifax, Nova Scotia.
[NRS.GD45.3.345/85-88]

BEAVOR, JOHN, born 1710, from Kingsale, Ireland, died 31 July 1768, husband of Honor ... from Montserrat. [St George gravestone, Basse Terre, St Kitts]

BELLEW, FRANCIS, formerly of St Kitts, but of Cork, will 1773. [PWI]

BENNETT, THOMAS, in Nevis, 1677-1678. [TNA]

BENNETT, THOMAS, a founder member of the Irish Charitable Society of Boston in 1736. [UJA.II.1.18]

BETTS, THOMAS, in St Thomas, Middle Island, St Kitts on 7 February 1678. [TNA.COI.42]

BETTY, JOHN, in Montserrat in 1677-1678. [TNA]

BIRCH, THOMAS LEDLIE, emigrated from Belfast to New York in 1798. ['A letter from an Irish Emigrant .....', {New York, 1798}]

BLACK, JOHN, a planter in Trinidad, letters, 1797-1810. [PRONI.D4457]

BLACK, MOSES, President of the Irish Charitable Society of Boston in 1784. [UJA.II.1.18]

BLAIR, JAMES, in St Eustatius, accounts and letters, 1780-1795; a merchant in Barbados and Demerara, a letter and an account book, 1796-1799. [PRONI.DOD.717/19-27; 1125]

BLAKE, Mrs ANNE MARGARET HUME, born 1771, widow of Reverend Edward Burke Blake rector of Loughbrickland and Killegan, County Wicklow, with her two sons Reverend Dominick Edward Blake and William Hume Blake and their wives, emigrated to Canada aboard the Ann of Halifax in 1832. [PRONI.Mic.205.1]

BLAKE, BRYAN, a merchant in Antigua, will, 1801. [PWI]

BLAKE, MARTIN, in Montserrat in 1677-1678. [TNA]

BLEAKLEY, JOHN, of the Island of St Croix, will, 1804. [PWI]

BODKIN, ANDREW, third brother of Edmond Bodkin late of Kilaloony, County Galway, married Margaret Denn of St Croix, Danish West Indies, there in 1770. [FLJ.65]

BODKIN, THOMAS, in the parish of Sandy Point, St Kitts on 7 February 1678. [TNA.COI.42]

BODKIN, THOMAS, a land-owner at English Harbor, Antigua, 1744. [JCTP.66.186]

BOHELY, JOHN, in Montserrat in 1677-1678. [TNA]

BONNY, THOMAS, in Montserrat in 1677-1678. [TNA]

BORKE, DAVID, in Montserrat in 1677-1678. [TNA]

BOSKEN, JAMES, in Montserrat in 1677-1678. [TNA]

BOURK, BRYAN, born 1616, emigrated via London aboard the Ann and Elizabeth, master John Brookehaven, bound for Barbados in April 1635. [TNA.E157.20]

BOURKE, JOHN, a merchant at Black River on the Mosquito Shore in America, deed, 1772. [NRS.GD77.165]

BOYD, ADAM, a founder member of the Irish Charitable Society of Boston in 1736. [UJA.II.1.18]

BOYD, WILLIAM, minister of Macosquin, County Londonderry, bound for New England in 1718.

BOYLAN, JOHN, settled in Newport, William Boylan, [died 1913], and his wife Elizabeth, [1842-1922], grandson of James and Mary Smith. [Termonfeckin gravestone, County Louth]

BOYLE, PATRICK, emigrated from Sligo on 25 April 1847 aboard the Aeolus of Greenock bound for New Brunswick, landed at St John on 31 May 1847. [PANB.MC803]

BRADAN, HUGH, in Montserrat in 1677-1678. [TNA]

BRADLEY, WILLIAM, in Montserrat in 1677-1678. [TNA]

BRANNON, JAMES, born around 1733 in Ireland, an indentured servant who absconded in 1753.[VaGaz.4.1737]

BRATTLEY, HENRY, in the parish of St John Capistar, St Kitts, on 28 January 1678. [TNA.COI.42]

BRENNAN, DENNIS, in Montserrat in 1677-1678. [TNA]

BRENNAN, JAMES, born 1695 in County Carlow, died in Antigua on 24 September 1743. [St John's Cathedral, Antigua]

BRENNAN, JOHN, in Montserrat in 1677-1678. [TNA]

BRISKETT, ANTHONY, born in Wexford, a Governor of Montserrat in 16...[SPAWI]

BRISLANE, JAMES, in Montserrat in 1677-1678. [TNA]

BROADHURST, JOSEPH, in Antigua, will, 1737. [PWI]

BROGAN, NICOLAS, born 1607, emigrated via London aboard the Expedition, master Peter Blackler, bound for Barbados in November 1635. [TNA.E157.20]

BROOKS, JAMES, born 1753, a linen weaver from Cork, via London aboard the Baltimore bound for Baltimore as a redemptioner in 1775. [TNA.T47.9/11]

BROWNE, Lieutenant HENRY, in Louisbourg, Nova Scotia, letters, 1759. [NLI.18444]

BROWN, JOHN, born in Belfast, formerly a merchant in Dublin, was captured by the French when on passage from Antigua, died on Marie Galante Island in the West Indies in September 1808. [GM.78.1126]

BROWNE, JOHN, possibly from County Clare, in Bathurst, New Brunswick, letters, 1843-1849. [NLI.20628] [PANB.MC3028]

BROWNE, PATRICK, in Montserrat in 1677-1678. [TNA]

BROWN, ROBERT, born 1762 in Springtown, Ireland, an Assemblyman of St Vincent, died 20 October 1830. [St Vincent monumental inscription]

IRISH EMIGRANTS IN NORTH AMERICA, Volume 9

BROWN, SAMUEL, from Cork, a merchant in Nevis, probate 1712, PCC. [TNA]

BROWN, WILLIAM, Captain of the 33rd Regiment at Boston, will, 1776. [PWI]

BROWNRIGG, JOHN, formerly in Jamaica, late in Dublin, will, 1792. [PWI]

BRUNNAN, CHRISTOPHER, a soldier of the 2nd Battalion of the 84th Regiment, commanded by Major John Small, aboard the frigate Raleigh, Captain Gambier, from New York bound for Charleston, South Carolina, in 1780. [NRS.GD174.2405]

BRUNNAN, PETER, a soldier of the 2nd Battalion of the 84th Regiment, commanded by Major John Small, aboard the frigate Raleigh, Captain Gambier, from New York bound for Charleston, South Carolina, in 1780. [NRS.GD174.2405]

BRIAN, CORNELIUS, in Montserrat in 1677-1678. [TNA]

BRYAN, DANIEL, in Montserrat in 1677-1678. [TNA]

BRYAN, PETER, in Montserrat in 1677-1678. [TNA]

BRYAN, RICHARD, in Montserrat in 1677-1678. [TNA]

BRYAN, THURLEIGH, in Montserrat in 1677-1678. [TNA]

BRYAN, THURLOGH, in the parish of Sandy Point, St Kitts on 7 February 1678. [TNA.COI.42]

BRYANT, THURLOGH in Halfwaytree Division, St Kitts on 7 February 1678. [TNA.COI.42]

BRYAN, MICHAEL, in Montserrat in 1677-1678. [TNA]

BRYSON, ANDREW, from Bangor, County Down, a soldier on St Pierre, later in New York, an account dated 1801. [PRONI.T1373]

BRYAN, MORRIS, in Montserrat in 1677-1678. [TNA]

BUCHANAN, SAMUEL, [1837-1905], in America, 32 letters between 1870 and 1903. [NLI.Buchanan Papers]

BUCKELLY, THOMAS, a pedlar from Wexford, a soldier of the 58th Regiment of Foot, was found guilty of robbing an officer's quarters in Quebec and was sentenced to 1000 lashes. [TNA.WO71.46/10-14; WO25.435.67]

BURK, REDMOND, in Montserrat in 1677-1678. [TNA]

BURKE, EDMUND, born 1756, a priest in Placentia, Newfoundland, from 1786 until 1800, later in Nova Scotia

BURKE, JAMES, formerly of Ireland, late of Pennsylvania, will, 1807. [PWI]

BURK, JONATHAN, in Montserrat in 1677-1678. [TNA]

BURKE, PATRICK JOHN, a gentleman in Kingston, Jamaica, an indenture, 15 May 1779. [Caribeanna.3.25]

BURKE, DENIS, MD, born 1752, late assistant surgeon at West Point, died in Washington on 29 June 1852. [GM.ns38.433]

BURKE, RICHARD, in Montserrat in 1677-1678. [TNA]

BURKE, WILLIAM, a soldier stationed at Placentia, Newfoundland, in 1732. [TNA.CO194.24.109]

BURKELY, DENNIS, in Montserrat in 1677-1678. [TNA]

BURN, BRYAN, born 1753 in Ireland, a husbandman and an indentured servant, bound via London aboard the Hawk for Philadelphia in 1775. [TNA.T47.9/11]

BURNS, JOHN, a soldier of the 2nd Battalion of the 84th Regiment, commanded by Major John Small, aboard the frigate Raleigh, Captain Gambier, from New York bound for Charleston, South Carolina, in 1780. [NRS.GD174.2405]

BURNS, MATTHEW, born 1810, son of William Burns and his wife Susanna .... In Belfast, died 1850 in Jamaica. [New Burying Ground gravestone, Belfast]

BUSHE, JOHN SCOTT, eldest son of the late Robert Bushe in Dublin, married Martha Macnamara Cummings, eldest daughter of Archdeacon Cummings, and grandniece of the late Admiral Macnamara, in Port of Spain, Trinidad, on 6 June 1848. [GM.ns30.199]

BUTLER, CHARLES, in Philadelphia, mate of the ship Polly, will, 1777. [PWI]

BUTLER, GERARD, born 1608, emigrated via London aboard the David, master John Hogg, bound for Virginia in September 1635. [TNA.E157.20]

BUTLER, JAMES, in Montserrat in 1677-1678. [TNA]

BUTLER, JAMES, in Boston, a letter, 16 September 1678. [NLI.MS2377]

BUTLER, JAMES, a planter at Harbour Main, Newfoundland, 1819. [TNA.CO194.64.6-12]

BUTLER, KATHERINE, born 1654 in Sligo, died in Antigua on 6 May 1735. [St John's Cathedral, Antigua]

BUTLER, Captain THOMAS, in Nevis or St Kitts, probate 1689, PCC. [TNA]

BUTLER, THOMAS, in Nevis or St Kitts, probate 1744, PCC. [TNA]

BUTLER, TOBIAS, in Montserrat in 1677-1678. [TNA]

BUTLER, TOBIAS, in the parish of Sandy Point, St Kitts on 7 February 1678. [TNA.COI.42]

BYNN, FRANCIS, in Montserrat in 1677-1678. [TNA]

BYRNE, GARRETT, in Elizabeth-town, North America, will, 1789. [PWI]

BYRNE, WILLIAM, a bookseller, son of Patrick Byrne a bookseller in Dublin, died in Philadelphia on 21 December 1805. [GM.76.182]

CAFFREY, THURLOGH, in Montserrat in 1677-1678. [TNA]

CAGAN, BRIAN, born around 1688 in Ireland, an indentured servant who absconded from his master in Richmond County, Virginia, in 1738. [VaGaz; June 1738]

CAHANE, HENRY, in Montserrat in 1677-1678. [TNA]

CAHESIE, TEIGE, in Montserrat in 1677-1678. [TNA]

CAHILL, DERBY, in Montserrat in 1677-1678. [TNA]

CAHILL, JOHN M., [1840-1928], born Templeglantine, County Limerick, emigrated to America in 1863, settled in Pearwater, Michigan, writer of prose and verses in Gaelic. [NLI.MSS510/529/543]

CAHOSY, EDMOND, in Montserrat in 1677-1678. [TNA]

CALDWELL, GEORGE, emigrated via Londonderry aboard the snow Frodsham, master James Aspinall, bound for Philadelphia in 1735, sought in 1740. [PaGaz.5.6.1740]

CALDWELL, HENRY, born in Ireland, a Colonel in the British Army during the Seven Years War, [1756-1763], later the Receiver General of Quebec.

CALLAHAN, CORNELIUS, in Montserrat in 1677-1678. [TNA]

CALLAHAN, DENNIS in Halfwaytree Division, St Kitts on 7 February 1678. [TNA.COI.42]

CALLAHAN, DENNIS, in Montserrat in 1677-1678. [TNA]

CALLAHAN, DERMOND in Halfwaytree Division, St Kitts on 7 February 1678. [TNA.COI.42]

CALLAHAN, JOHN, in Montserrat in 1677-1678. [TNA]

CAMAC, WILLIAM, born 1804 in Greenmount, County Down, died in Philadelphia on 7 March 1842. [GM.ns17.678]

CAMPBELL, THOMAS, settled as a merchant in Philadelphia by 1728. [PaGaz.21.1.1729]

CANANA, DARBY, in Montserrat in 1677-1678. [TNA]

CANARAN, TEIGE, in the parish of Sandy Point, St Kitts on 7 February 1678. [TNA.COI.42]

CANAVANE, DAVID, in the parish of Sandy Point, St Kitts on 7 February 1678. [TNA.COI.42]

CANAVAN, JOHN, in the parish of Sandy Point, St Kitts on 7 February 1678. [TNA.COI.42]

CANAVAN, Sergeant WILLIAM, in Montserrat 1677-1678. [TNA]

CANNELLY, DANIEL, born 1615, emigrated via London aboard the Amity, master George Downes, bound for St Kitts in October 1635. [TNA.E157.20]

CANTELLY, LUKE, in Montserrat in 1677-1678. [TNA]

CARAM, JOHN, in the parish of Sandy Point, St Kitts on 7 February 1678. [TNA.COI.42]

CARRE, HENRY, eldest son of Reverend Carre in Raphoe, Ireland, married Louis de Quincy Lundy, third daughter of Reverend F J Lundy of Grimsby, Upper Canada, in Stirling, Upper Canada, on 9 August 1866. [GM.ns3.2.539]

CARRELAM, PATRICK, in Montserrat in 1677-1678. [TNA]

CARROLL, DANIEL, in Montserrat in 1677-1678. [TNA]

CARROLL, HUGH, died in America, son of Patrick Carroll, born 1788, died 7 August 1867, and Bridget Carroll. [Termonfeckin gravestone, County Louth]

CARROLL, ROGER, in Montserrat in 1677-1678. [TNA]

CARSAN, ROBERT, a merchant in Philadelphia, will, 1784. [PWI]

CARTY, CHARLES, in Montserrat in 1677-1678. [TNA]

CARTY, DANIEL, in St Thomas, Middle Island, St Kitts on 7 February 1678. [TNA.COI.42]

CARTY, DENNIS, in Montserrat in 1677-1678. [TNA]

CARTY, DENNIS in St Thomas, Middle Island, St Kitts on 7 February 1678. [TNA.COI.42]

CARTY, FLORENCE, in Montserrat in 1677-1678. [TNA]

CARTY, GILBERT, born 1754, a farmer from Ireland, via London aboard the Adventure bound for Maryland as a redemptioner in 1775. [TNA.T47.9/11]

CARTY, OWEN, in Montserrat in 1677-1678. [TNA]

CARTY, TEIGE, in Montserrat in 1677-1678. [TNA]

CARTY, TYMOTHY, in the parish of St John Capistar, St Kitts, on 28 January 1678. [TNA.COl.42]

CARY, JOHN, from Munster, Ireland, an indentured servant bound from Bristol to the Plantations on 7 May 1658. [BRO]

CASEY, JOHN in Halfwaytree Division, St Kitts on 7 February 1678. [TNA.COl.42]

CASEY, SIMON, in Halfwaytree Division, St Kitts on 7 February 1678. [TNA.COl.42]

CASSEDY, JOHN, born 1615, emigrated via London aboard the Hopewell, master Thomas Wood, bound for Barbados in February 1635. [TNA.E157.20]

CASSY, MORRIS, in Montserrat in 1677-1678. [TNA]

CASTALLO, JORDAN, born 1744, a clerk from Dublin, via London aboard the Fortune bound for Maryland in 1775, as an indentured servant. [TNA.T47.9/11]

CAVENAGH, HUGH, a yeoman, emigrated via Bristol bound for Virginia in August 1658. [BRO]

CHABERT, ANDREW, in the Island of St Croix, will, 1801. [PWI]

CHALMERS, JOHN, from Belfast, settled in Antigua, a letter, 1731. [PRONI.D162.24]

CHECKLEY, Reverend JOHN, born 31 March 1789 in Cork, was educated at Trinity College, Dublin, died 6 January 1852. [St Vincent gravestone]

CHRYSTAL, HUGH, emigrated from Sligo on 25 April 1847 aboard the Aeolus of Greenock bound for New Brunswick, landed at St John on 31 May 1847. [PANB.MC803]

CLARKE, A., born 1763, from Trinidad, died in Belmont, County Donegal, on 16 April 1836. [GM..ns6.110]

CLARKE, HENRIETTA JANE, second daughter of Lieutenant General St John A. Clarke, Dublin, married H. Compton Best, a Lieutenant of the Royal Navy, second son of George Best in Surrey, in Halifax, Nova Scotia, on 25 July 1865. [GM.ns2/19.373]

CLARK, JAMES, a founder member of the Irish Charitable Society of Boston in 1736. [UJA.II.1.18]

CLARK, JOHN, a founder member of the Irish Charitable Society of Boston in 1736. [UJA.II.1.18]

CLARKE, SIMON, in Jamaica, a letter, 1754. [PRONI.DOD.162/70]

CLEARY, EDMOND, in Montserrat in 1677-1678. [TNA]

CLEARY, OWEN, in Montserrat in 1677-1678. [TNA]

CLEMENTS, JANE, born 1683, a spinster from Dublin, emigrated via Liverpool to America in 1704. [LRO]

CLONANE, MORRIS, in Montserrat in 1677-1678. [TNA]

CLUNE, THOMAS, from Munster, an indentured servant bound via London for Jamaica in 1753. [CLRO.ASP.6]

COCHRAN, JOSEPH, died in Pennsylvania in 1727. [Chester County inventory 285]

COCKERANCE, EDWARD, at St John's, Newfoundland, in 1752. [TNA.CO194.13.55]

COGAN, DAVID, in Montserrat in 1677-1678. [TNA]

COGAN, HENRY, with his wife, emigrated via Weymouth aboard the Speedwell, master Robert Corbin, bound for New England in April 1637. [TNA.E190.876.11]

COGAN, JOHN, in the parish of Sandy Point, St Kitts on 7 February 1678. [TNA.COI.42]

COGHALL, THOMAS, in the parish of Sandy Point, St Kitts on 7 February 1678. [TNA.COI.42]

COHANE, BRYAN, in Montserrat in 1677-1678. [TNA]

COLDMAIN, JAMES, in Montserrat in 1677-1678. [TNA]

COLLINS, JOHN, in Montserrat in 1677-1678. [TNA]

COLLINS, MAURICE, an indentured servant, emigrated from Cork aboard the brig Pattie bound for Philadelphia in 1773. [PaGaz:24.11.1773]

COLLINS, THOMAS, Captain of HM 11th West India Regiment, will, 1802. [PWI]

COLLY, PHILIP, in Montserrat in 1677-1678. [TNA]

CONDON, DAVID, in Montserrat in 1677-1678. [TNA]

CONDEN, MORRIS in Halfwaytree Division, St Kitts on 7 February 1678. [TNA.COI.42]

CONDON, MORRIS, in Montserrat in 1677-1678. [TNA]

CONEADE, TEIGE, in the parish of Sandy Point, St Kitts on 7 February 1678. [TNA.COI.42]

CONNELL, DARBY, a soldier of the 2nd Battalion of the 84th Regiment, commanded by Major John Small, aboard the frigate Raleigh, Captain Gambier, from New York bound for Charleston, South Carolina, in 1780. [NRS.GD174.2405]

CONNELL, JAMES, a tavern-keeper in Kingston, Jamaica, will, 1720. [PWI]

CONNELL, JOHN, in Montserrat in 1677-1678. [TNA]

CONNELL, REDMOND, a soldier of the 2nd Battalion of the 84th Regiment, commanded by Major John Small, aboard the frigate Raleigh, Captain Gambier, from New York bound for Charleston, South Carolina, in 1780. [NRS.GD174.2405]

CONNELL, TEIGE, in Kayon Division, St Kitts on 7 February 1678. [TNA.COI.42]

CONNER, ARTHUR, in the parish of Sandy Point, St Kitts on 7 February 1678. [TNA.COI.42]

CONNER, DANIEL, in Montserrat in 1677-1678. [TNA]

CONNER, JOHN, in Montserrat in 1677-1678. [TNA]

CONNOR, LAWRENCE, a husbandman from Dublin, an indentured servant bound via London for Virginia in April 1752. [CLRO.ASP.5]

CONNER, PATRICK in St Thomas, Middle Island, St Kitts on 7 February 1678. [TNA.COI.42]

CONNER, TEIGE, in Kayon Division, St Kitts on 7 February 1678. [TNA.COl.42]

CONNERY, WILLIAM, in the parish of St John Capistar, St Kitts, on 28 January 1678. [TNA.COl.42]

CONNOR, HUGH, in Montserrat in 1677-1678. [TNA]

CONNOR, JOHN, a soldier of the 2nd Battalion of the 84th Regiment, commanded by Major John Small, aboard the frigate Raleigh, Captain Gambier, from New York bound for Charleston, South Carolina, in 1780. [NRS.GD174.2405]

CONNOE, EDMOND, in Montserrat in 1677-1678. [TNA]

CONSYDEN, DERMOND, in the parish of Sandy Point, St Kitts on 7 February 1678. [TNA.COl.42]

CONSYDEN, JOHN, in the parish of Sandy Point, St Kitts on 7 February 1678. [TNA.COl.42]

CONYNGHAM, JAMES BARBER, of Belfast and Barbados, a will, subscribed 1843. [PRONI.T700.1]

CONYNGHAM, SAMUEL, of Belfast and Barbados, a will subscribed 1783. [PRONI.T700.1]

CONWAY, PATRICK, at Placentia, Newfoundland, a petitioner, 1744. [TNA.CO194.24.298]

CONWAY, WILLIAM, in Montserrat in 1677-1678. [TNMA]

COOKE, ELLA, youngest daughter of Michael Cooke of Palatine House, County Carlow married Alexander McCombie the younger, eldest son of Alexander McCombie, in Trinity Church, Castries, St Lucia, British West Indies, on 20 March 1851. [AJ.5390]

COOKE, JOHN, in the parish of Overwharton, County Stafford, Virginia, will, 1735. [PWI]

CORMACK, Lieutenant Colonel, JOHN, a planter and Colonel of Militia, with 4 women and 4 children, on Montserrat in 1677. [TNA]

CORMACK, Ensign JOHN, in Montserrat in 1677-1678. [TNA]

CORMODY, DANIEL, in Montserrat in 1677-1678. [TNA]

CORNYN, DOMINICK, in Jamaica, surgeon of the galley John, will, 1755. [PWI]

CORRUE, TEIGE, in Montserrat in 1677-1678. [TNA]

CORRY, JAMES, emigrated from Ireland to America by 1776, settled in Cooksburg, Albany County, New York, a Loyalist in 1776, a soldier in Roger's Corps of the King's Rangers, settled in Canada in 1782, died in Lancaster township before 1788. [TNA.AO12.33.13]

COSBY, Sir WILLIAM, born 1690 in Strabally, Queen's County, a professional soldier, Governor of New York from 1732 until hi death in 1736.

COSGRAVE, JAMES, in Antigua, will, 1765. [PWI]

COSSLY, JAMES, in the parish of Sandy Point, St Kitts on 7 February 1678. [TNA.COI.42]

COSSLY, JAMES, in the parish of Sandy Point, St Kitts on 7 February 1678. [TNA.COI.42]

COSTELLO, MICHAEL, a surgeon in Jamaica, will, 1762, [PWI]

COTTER, JAMES, in Montserrat in 1677-1678. [TNA]

COTTON, MICHAEL, born 1745, a locksmith from Dublin, via London aboard the Fortune bound for Maryland as an indentured servant in 1775. [TNA.T47.9/11]

COUGHLAND, DERMOND, in the parish of Sandy Point, St Kitts on 7 February 1678. [TNA.COI.42]

COUGHLAN, LAWRENCE, a Methodist preacher at Harbour Grace, Newfoundland, in 1760s. [SPG.London ms.b6169/170]

COULTER, JAMES, from Banbridge, County Down, settled on Pequea Creek, Lancaster County, Pennsylvania, later died at sea aboard the John and Margaret in 1735. [Lancaster County Wills a-1.23]

COYLE, CHARLES, born 1739 in County Tyrone, a soldier of the 43rd Foot, fought in the St Lawrence campaign. [TNA.WO.121.6]

CRAFFORD, ALEXANDER, a gentleman in Antigua, will, 1730. [PWI]

CRAWFORD, GEORGE, Major of the 2nd West India Regiment, will, 1808. [PWI]

CRAWFORD, JANE, second daughter of Reverend Alexander Crawford in Main Mount, Randalstown, married James Gall of Jamaica, in Antrim on 13 June 1859. [CM.21754]

CRAWFORD, ..., emigrated from Londonderry aboard the Ardent bound for Baltimore in 1803. [NEHGR.LX.163]

CRAWLEY, JAMES, at Placentia, Newfoundland, a petitioner, 1744. [TNA.CO194.24.298]

CREALY, DENNIS, in Montserrat in 1677-1678. [TNA]

CRONANE, TEIGE, in Montserrat in 1677-1678. [TNA]

CRONEEN, JOHN in Halfwaytree Division, St Kitts on 7 February 1678. [TNA.COI.42]

CROWLY, TEIGE, in Montserrat in 1677-1678. [TNA]

CROVEEN, DANIEL, in Montserrat in 1677-1678. [TNA]

CULLENANE, OWEN, in Montserrat in 1677-1678. [TNA]

CULLNAGHTEN, JAMES, in Montserrat in 1677-1678. [TNA]

CUMMINGS, MARTHA MACNAMARA, eldest daughter of Archdeacon Cummings, and grand-niece of Admiral Macnamara, married John Scott Bushe, eldest son of Robert Bushe in Dublin, in Port of Spain, Trinidad, on 6 June 1848. [GM.ns30.199]

CUNEGAN, DANIELL, in Montserrat in 1677-1678. [TNA]

CUNIGAN, PATRICK, emigrated from Londonderry aboard the Ardent bound for Baltimore, Maryland, in 1803. [NEHGR.LX.163]

CUNNINGHAM, JOHN, from Belfast to Boston, a journal 1795-1796. [PRONI.D394.2]

CUNNINGHAM, SAMUEL, jr, of St Vincent and Martinique, letters relating to his will and estate, 1796-1828. [PRONI.DOD.1108/3-11, 16-27]

CUNNINGHAM, WALTER, a North Carolina Loyalist, will, 1789. [PWI]

CUNNINGHAM, WILLIAM, emigrated to America in 1757, a planter in Colleton County, South Carolina, a Loyalist in 1776, moved to Jamaica in 1783. [TNA.AO12.49.30, etc]

CURRAN, DAVID, from Dublin, an indentured servant, aboard the Eleanor, master Nicholas Reynolds, at Liverpool bound for Virginia or Maryland in February 1699. [LRO]

CURRAN, PATRICK, in Lower Canada, 1827. [NRS.GD45.3.534.8]

CURTIN, JOHN, a former 'horse rider' from County Cork, born 1695, a soldier of the 48th Regiment of Foot, was discharged at Crown Point, New York, on 20 October 1763, was granted land near Lake Champlain, dispossessed as a Loyalist in 1780. [TNA.WO116.9; AO12.102.130; AO13.97-98]

CUSEN, WILLIAM, in Montserrat in 1677-1678. [TNA]

CUSHEN, THOMAS, in the parish of St John Capistar, St Kitts, on 28 January 1678. [TNA.COl.42]

DALY, ANDREW, in Port Royal, Jamaica, will, 1735. [PWI]

DALLY, DANIEL, in Montserrat in 1677-1678. [TNA]

DALLY, DENNIS, in Montserrat in 1677-1678. [TNA]

DALEY, DENNIS, born 1723, an indentured servant who absconded from Amity, Philadelphia County, Pennsylvania, in 1745. [PaGaz:18.4.1745]

DALEY, Lieutenant EDMOND, in Montserrat in 1677-1678. [TNA]

DALY, JOHN, in Montserrat in 1677-1678. [TNA]

DALLY, JOHN, in Montserrat in 1677-1678. [TNA]

DALY, WILLIAM, a tory who surrendered, taken to Dublin, to be transported beyond the sea, 19 October 1669. [CSPI.1669]

DANIELL, JOHN, in the parish of Sandy Point, St Kitts on 7 February 1678. [TNA.COI.42]

DANIELL, RICHARD, in Montserrat in 1677-1678. [TNA]

DANIELL, THOMAS, in Montserrat in 1677-1678. [TNA]

DARBY, MICHAEL, born 1745, an indentured servant who absconded from Mr Burns' schooner in Charleston Harbor, South Carolina in April 1767. [SCGaz:12.4.1767]

DARCY, GARRATT, in the parish of Sandy Point, St Kitts on 7 February 1678. [TNA.COI.42]

DARCY, JOHN, in Montserrat in 1677-1678. [TNA]

DARCY, MATHEW, in Montserrat in 1677-1678. [TNA]

DARCY, PATRICK, in Montserrat in 1677-1678. [TNA]

DARCY, PETER, in Montserrat in 1677-1678. [TNA]

DARCY, RICHARD, in Montserrat in 1677-1678. [TNA]

DASHALL, WILLIAM, born 1751 in Ireland, from London aboard the *Maryland Planter* bound for Maryland in 1775. [TNA.T47.9/11]

DAUNT, JAMES, in Montserrat in 1677-1678. [TNA]

DAVIS, JONAS, from Cork, an indentured servant bound from Liverpool to America in 1698. [LRO]

DAVIS, THOMAS, foreman in HM Dockyard in Antigua, will, 1790. [PWI]

DAWSON, JAMES HEWITT MASSY, from Ireland, married Miss Dennis, eldest daughter of the late Francis Dawson, in Jamaica on 11 March 1800. [GM.70.282]

DAY, JAMES, from Dublin, aboard the Planter, master John Rimmer, bound for Newfoundland from Liverpool in March 1699. [LRO]

DEADY, Captain, of Cork, 'several years on the West India trade', died in Dominica in 1765. [FDJ.4023]

DELANY, DENNIS, a soldier of the 2nd Battalion of the 84th Regiment, commanded by Major John Small, aboard the frigate Raleigh, Captain Gambier, from New York bound for Charleston, South Carolina, in 1780. [NRS.GD174.2405]

DELANEY, JOHN, settled at McLellan's Mountain, East River, Pictou County, Nova Scotia, in 1794, there with three children in 1809. [NSARM.RG20,Series A]

DELANEY, RICHARD MAR, born 1753, son of Daniel M. Delaney and his wife Mary, died 31 March 1755, also son Daniel born 1753, died 26 November 1757, and the above Mrs Mary Delaney, born 1720, died 9 May 1783. [St George gravestone, Basse Terre, St Kitts]

DELARCY, MORRIS, in Montserrat in 1677-1678. [TNA]

DEMPSEY, RICHARD, in Montserrat in 1677-1678. [TNA]

DENNIN, CHARLES, in the parish of Sandy Point, St Kitts on 7 February 1678. [TNA.COl.42]

DENNIS, THURLOUGH, in Montserrat in 1677-1678.
[TNA]

DENNIS, Miss, eldest daughter of Francis Dennis in Jamaica, married James Hewitt Massy Dawson, in Ireland on 11 March 1800. [GM.70.282]

DERMOND, DENNIS, in Montserrat in 1677-1678. [TNA]

DERMOND, JOHN, in Montserrat in 1677-1678. [TNA]

DERMOND, TERENCE, in Montserrat in 1677-1678. [TNA]

DEVIN, JOHN, settled in Boston, USA, son of Patrick Devin, born 1817, died 27 July 1903, and his wife Ann Devin of Milltown, born 1815, died 27 March 1880. [Termonfeckin gravestone, County Louth]

DEWYER, ANTHONY, born 1755, a tailor from Cork, bound from Bristol aboard the Mary for Maryland in 1775 as an indentured servant. [TNA.T47.9/11]

DEXETER, GEORGE, in Montserrat in 1677-1678. [TNA]

DICKSON, H., in Mexico, a letter, 1916. [PRONI.DOD.1078/F.47]

DINGLE, JAMES, in the parish of Sandy Point, St Kitts on 7 February 1678. [TNA.COI.42]

DOCHERTY, FELIX, died in St Jan, Danish West Indies, on 29 February 1832, probate, St Jan, 1826-1836, fo.107.

DOCHERTY, MARTIN, died in St Jan, Danish West Indies, on 21 June 1827, probate, St Jan, 1826-1836, fos. 20-25.

DOGHARTY, JOHN, born 1752, a surgeon from Ireland, in Polly bound for Maryland in 1774. [TNA.T47.9/11]

DOLE, JAMES, in Nevis, 1677-1678. [TNA]

D'OLIER, THEOPHILIUS, a merchant from Dublin, died 22 November 18-9. [St Michael's Cathedral gravestone, Barbados]

DOLLANE, JAMES, in Montserrat in 1677-1678. [TNA]

DOLLY, DANIEL, in Montserrat in 1677-1678. [TNA]

DOLOGHERY, JOHN, in Montserrat in 1677-1678. [TNA]

DONALDSON, HUGH, a gentleman, formerly of Philadelphia, late in Drumnasole, County Antrim, will, 1774, refers to William Agnew in Kilwaughter, Hugh McCollum in Liminary, William Burgess a merchant in Belfast, all in County Antrim, wits. Valentine Jones a merchant in Belfast, Robert Harrison a gentleman in Dublin, Thomas Elder a merchant in Belfast, Samuel Ashmore a merchant in Belfast. [DRD]

DONAHUL, OWEN, in Montserrat in 1677-1678. [TNA]

DONN, RICHARD, in the parish of St John Capistar, St Kitts, on 28 January 1678. [TNA.COI.42]

DONNELAN, PATRICK, a planter in Jamaica, will, 1801. [PWI]

DONNALL, JOHN, at the Glen near Larne, emigrated to Philadelphia in 1766. [BNL:22.4.1766]

DONOUGH, JOHN, in Montserrat in 1677-1678. [TNA]

DONOVAN, DANIEL, in Montserrat in 1677-1678. [TNA]

DONOVAN, DARBY, a soldier of the 2nd Battalion of the 84th Regiment, commanded by Major John Small, aboard the frigate Raleigh, Captain Gambier, from New York bound for Charleston, S.C. in 1780. [NRS.GD174.2405]

DONOVAN, DERMOND, in Kayon Division, St Kitts on 7 February 1678. [TNA.COl.42]

DONOVAN, LAWRENCE, late Deputy Commissary General of Barbados, died at St Stephen's Green, Dublin in 1820. [F.J.4.2.1820]

DONAVAN, TEIGE, in Montserrat in 1677-1678. [TNA]

DORANE, TEIGE, in Montserrat in 1677-1678. [TNA]

DORNEY, OWEN, in Montserrat in 1677-1678. [TNA]

DOUGHERTY, EDWARD, an inn-keeper in Donegal, Pennsilvania, 1731. [Lancaster County Quarter Sessions; 4 May 1731]

DOUGHERTY, JOHN, a cordwainer from Dublin, a solder of the 58th Regiment of Foot, was found guilty of robbing an officer's quarters in Quebec, and was sentenced to 1000 lashes. [TNA.WO71.46/10-14; WO25.435/67]

DOWDY, Sergeant DANIEL, in Montserrat in 1677-1678. [TNA]

DOWDY, DERMOND, in Montserrat in 1677-1678. [TNA]

DOWDY, FARRELL, in Montserrat in 1677-1678. [TNA]

DOWDY, JOHN, sr. & jr., in Montserrat in 1677-1678. [TNA]

DOWDY, OWEN, in Montserrat in 1677-1678. [TNA]

DOWLING, JOHN, son of John Dowling a timber merchant in Back Lane, Dublin, died in Jamaica, in 1765. [FDJ.3965]

DOWNS, DANIEL, born 1740, an indentured servant who absconded in Pennsylvania on 17 June 1770. [PaGaz:19.6.1770]

DOYLE, ANDREW, in the West Indies, a letter around 1728. [HMC.55.Var.Coll.viii]

DOYLE, JAMES, from County Carlow, and Janet Fraser from Inverness-shire, were married in Halifax, Nova Scotia, on 10 February 1835. [Acadian Recorder: 14.2.1835]

DOYLE, MICHAEL, a soldier of the 2nd Battalion of the 84th Regiment, commanded by Major John Small, aboard the frigate Raleigh, Captain Gambier, from New York bound for Charleston, South Carolina, in 1780. [NRS.GD174.2405]

DRADY, FRANCIS, in Montserrat in 1677-1678. [TNA]

DRISCOLL, DANIEL, in Montserrat in 1677-1678. [TNA]

DRISCOLL, DERMOND, in Montserrat in 1677-1678. [TNA]

DRISCOLL, MICHAEL, in St John, New Brunswick, a letter, 1847, possibly arrived from Sligo aboard the Aeolus of Greenock. [PANB.MC803]

DRISCOLL, TERGE, in Nevis, 1677-1678. [TNA]

DRUMMOND, WILLIAM, a founder member of the Irish Charitable Society of Boston in 1736. [UJA.II.1.18]

DUANE, ANTHONY, born in County Galway, a merchant in New York in 17

DUME, JOHN, in Montserrat in 1677-1678. [TNA]

DUNAVAND, DANIEL, with one woman, in Montserrat in 1677-1678. [TNA]

DUNAVAIN, NICHOLAS, with a woman and a child in Montserrat in 1677-1678. [TNA]

DUNBAR, CHARLES, from northern Ireland, settled in Antigua by 1731. [PRONI.D162.24]

DUNCAN, ROBERT, a founder member of the Irish Charitable Society of Boston, Massachusetts, in 1736. [UJA.II.1.18]

DUNDO, CORNELIUS, in Montserrat in 1677-1678. [TNA]

DUNLAP, JOHN, a printer from Strabane, County Tyrone, settled in Philadelphia, Pennsylvania, a letter, 1785. [PRONI.T1336.1.20]

DUNN, TEIGE, in Montserrat in 1677-1678. [TNA]

DUNN, THOMAS, second son of the late William Dunn a baker in Dublin, died in St Croix in 1798. [GM.68.724]

DUNOVAN, DENNIS, in St Thomas, Middle Island, St Kitts on 7 February 1678. [TNA.COI.42]

DUNNOVAN, JOHN, in Montserrat in 1677-1678. [TNA]

DYAS, ROBERT, an apothecary in Albany, New York, will, 1806. [PWI]

DYSART, FANNY, emigrated via Londonderry aboard the brig George bound for Philadelphia in September 1769. [Familia.22.33-50]

ECCLES, ANNA, eldest daughter of Captain Eccles of Dublin and Bath, married John Bower Lewis, in Niagara on 17 October 1840. [GM.ns15.90]

ECCLES, JAMES, from Lough Lavin in Ireland, an indentured servant aboard the Ann and Sarah master John Marshall, bound from Liverpool for America in 1698. [LRO]

EEDY, PATRICK, from Bandon, County Cork, settled in Bathurst, New Brunswick, and in St Peter's, Nova Scotia, by 1827. [CA.CCCA.U9]

EEDY, WILLIAM, in Clifton, Gloucester County, New Brunswick, a letter, 1838. [CA.CCCA.U9]

EGART, JAMES, a founder member the Irish Charitable Society of Boston, Massachusetts, in 1736. [UJA.II.1.18]

EGAN, JOHN, in Montserrat in 1677-1678. [TNA]

ELDER, ROBERT, emigrated to Pennsylvania in 1772, moved to South Carolina in 1775, a Loyalist, returned to County Antrim after 1781. [TNA.AO12.48.195-200]

ELLIOTT, SAMUEL, President of the Irish Charitable Society of Boston, Massachusetts, in 1757. [UJA.II.1.18]

ELLIOTT, THOMAS, in Montserrat in 1677-1678. [TNA]

ELLIOT, ..., emigrated from Londonderry aboard the Ardent bound for Baltimore, Maryland, in 1803. [NEHGR.LX.163]

ELTON, C. B., son of the late Reverend J. Elton in Dublin, died in Philadelphia in 1802. [GM.72.785]

ELWAY, THOMAS, sr. and jr., in Montserrat in 1677-1678. [TNA]

EMMETT, Mr, a counsellor and projector of the Irish Rebellion of 1791, died in New York in 1827. [GM.97.647]

EMRANSON, SYLVESTER, from the West Indies, married Alice Exton in Ireland on 13 September 1747. [GM.17.447]

ESPINASSE, REUBEN, second son of Major Espinasse in Dundrum, County Dublin, married Madeline Josephine Ellen Gillmer, only daughter of J. T. Gillmer of Philadelphia, in Gravesend on 11 February 1868. [GM.ns3/5.387]

ERROLL, PEIRCE, in Montserrat in 1677-1678. [TNA]

EWER, THOMAS, born 1749 in Dublin, a priest at Conception Bay, Newfoundland, from 1788.

EXTON, ALICE, from Ireland, married Sylvester Emranson, in the West Indies on 13 September 1747. [GM.17.447]

FALLON, DANIEL, a planter in Montserrat in 1643. [CLRO, Deposition, 7.2.1655]

FALLWAY, TEIGE, in Montserrat in 1677-1678. [TNA]

FARRELL, RICHARD, in Montserrat in 1677-1678. [TNA]

FARREL, THOMAS, from Dublin, an indentured servant bound from Liverpool to America in 1698. [LRO]

FARRELL, WILLIAM, an indentured servant who absconded from London Grove, Charles County Pennsylvania, in July 1750. [PaGaz:16.8.1750]

FEENEY, BRYAN, emigrated from Sligo on 25 April 1847 aboard the Aeolus of Greenock bound for New Brunswick, landed at St John on 31 May 1847. [PANB.MC803]

FEENEY, PATRICK, emigrated from Sligo on 25 April 1847 aboard the Aeolus of Greenock bound for New Brunswick, landed at St John on 31 May 1847. [PANB.MC803]

FENAN, ROGER, in Montserrat in 1677-1678. [TNA]

FERGUSON, WILLIAM, emigrated from Sligo on 25 April 1847 aboard the Aeolus of Greenock bound for New Brunswick, landed at St John on 31 May 1847. [PANB.MC803]

FENGHEY, CHARLES, in Montserrat in 1677-1678. [TNA]

FERNS, JONATHAN GORE, former Major of the 76th Regiment, eldest son of the late T. Burgh Ferns of County Dublin, died in Halifax, Nova Scotia, on 26 May 1856. [GM.ns2.1.124]

FERRALL, MATHIAS, a planter on the island of St Croix, West Indies, will, 1787. [PWI]

FIELDING, PATRICK, a soldier of the 2nd Battalion of the 84th Regiment, commanded by Major John Small, aboard the frigate Raleigh, Captain Gambier, from New York bound for Charleston, South Carolina, in 1780. [NRS.GD174.2405]

FINNITY, CATHERINE, born 1753, an indentured servant who absconded from Newcastle County, Pennsylvania, on 20 December 1775. [PaGaz: 12.4.1776]

FINNITY, JOSEPH, a cooper, who absconded from
Newcastle County, Pennsylvania, on 2 April 1776.
[PaGaz:12.4.1776]

FINNY, DERMOND, in Montserrat in 1677-1678. [TNA]

FINNY, JOHN, in Montserrat in 1677-1678. [TNA]

FISHER, HUGH, formerly in Edenberry parish, County
Armagh, settled in South Carolina by 1725. [see Alexander
Hutcheson's will, 1725, Dublin Register of Deeds]

FITZGERALD, GIDEON, in Montserrat in 1677-1678.
[TNA]

FITZGARRALD, MAURICE, in the parish of Sandy
Point, St Kitts on 7 February 1678. [TNA.COl.42]

FITZGERALD, MICHAEL, a soldier of the 2nd Battalion
of the 84th Regiment, commanded by Major John Small,
aboard the frigate Raleigh, Captain Gambier, from New
York bound for Charleston, South Carolina, in 1780.
[NRS.GD174.2405]

FITZGERALD, WILLIAM, born 1737 in Ireland, a
labourer, was recruited in Boston, Massachusetts, in 1758
by Captain Cosnan of the 45th Regiment of Foot.
[NRS.GD45.2.24.4B]

FITZGERALD, ..., a soldier of the 2nd Battalion of the
84th Regiment, commanded by Major John Small,
aboard the frigate Raleigh, Captain Gambier, from New
York bound for Charleston, South Carolina, in 1780.
[NRS.GD174.2405]

FITZJAMES, THOMAS, a felon, transported from
Plymouth aboard the John, master John Cole, bound for
Barbados in March 1656. [Lord Mayor's Court
Deposition]

FITZMORRIS, JAMES, in Montserrat in 1677-1678. [TNA]

FITZSIMMONS, THOMAS a felon, transported from Plymouth aboard the John, master John Cole, bound for Barbados in March 1656. [Lord Mayor's Court Deposition]

FITZWILLIAM, RICHARD, Governor of the Bahama Islands, will, 1744. [PWI]

FLAWS, RICHARD, from Dublin, a surgeon in Maryland, will, 1675. [PWI]

FLEMING, Dr MICHAEL, Vicar Apostolic of Newfoundland, 14 letters, around 1838. [NLI.15054]

FLEMING, ROBERT, in the parish of Sandy Point, St Kitts on 7 February 1678. [TNA.COI. 42]

FLYN, ANDREW, a cooper from Fermanagh, a soldier of the 58th Regiment of Foot, was acquitted of robbery in Quebec, deserted on 22 January 1764. [TNA.WO25.435/67-8, 85-6]

FLYNN, WILLIAM, emigrated from Ireland to New York in 1763, a merchant on Nassau Street, New York, a Loyalist in 1776, settled in Halifax, Nova Scotia, by 1786. [TNA.AO12.102.96]

FLING, DANIEL, in Montserrat in 1677-1678. [TNA]

FLING, OWEN, in Montserrat in 1677-1678. [TNA]

FOGERTON, DANIEL, in the parish of Sandy Point, St Kitts on 7 February 1678. [TNA.COI. 42]

FORBES, JOHN, the Governor of the Bahamas, a barrister, former MP for Drogheda, died in Nassau, New Providence, on 13 June 1797. [GM.67.711]

FOREMAN, JOHN, born 1820, son of J. Foreman in Belfast, a merchant and assemblyman, died in Antigua on 14 June 1866. [GM.ns3.2.269]

FOWLER DANIEL, in Montserrat in 1677-1678. [TNA]

FOWLER, DENNIS, in Montserrat in 1677-1678. [TNA]

FOWLER, MORRIS, in Montserrat in 1677-1678. [TNA]

FOWLER, PETER, born 1722, an indentured servant who absconded from William Hartley in Charlestown, Chester County, Pennsylvania, on 23 February 1747. [PaGaz:3.3.1747]

FREELAND, WILLIAM, a founder member of the Irish Charitable Society of Boston, Massachusetts, in 1736. [UJA.II.1.18]

FREEMAN, THOMAS, in Antigua, will, 1736. [PWI]

FRENCH, GEORGE, in Montserrat in 1677-1678. [TNA]

FRENCH, JOHN, from Washford, Ireland, aged 26, emigrated via Dartmouth aboard the bound for St Kitts in 20 February 1634. [TNA]

FRENCH, PETER, in Montserrat in 1677-1678. [TNA]

GALWAY, DAVID, a planter in Montserrat, British West Indies, in the 1660s, Major of the Militia in Montserrat, a member of the Council of Montserrat in the 1670s. [TNA]

GALBRAITH, JOHN, settled in Donegal, Chester County, Pennsylvania, in 1721.

GALLOWAY, JOHN, in Montserrat in 1677-1678. [TNA]

GALLOHO, FARRELL, in Montserrat in 1677-1678. [TNA]

GAMBLE, HAMILTON V., born 1820, son of Robert Gamble [1776-1836] and his wife Anne..... [1763-1836], died in New Orleans in 1839. [New Burying Burying Ground gravestone, Belfast.]

GAMBLE, JOHN, born 1809, son of Robert Gamble [1776-1836] and his wife Anne ... [1763-1836], died in New Orleans in 1828. [New Burying Ground, Belfast]

GAMBLE, ROBERT, born 1806, died at Bunker's Hill, Illinois, in 1867, husband of Mary Dickson, born 1804, died in New Orleans in 1851. [New Burying Ground, Belfast]

GANAN, MOSETT, in Montserrat in 1677-1678. [TNA]

GANAN, THOMAS, in Montserrat in 1677-1678. [TNA]

GARRALD, EDMOND, in the parish of Sandy Point, St Kitts on 7 February 1678. [TNA.COI. 42]

GARVIN, CHRISTOPHER, in Montserrat in 1677-1678. [TNA]

GARVIN, JAMES, from Castletownroche, emigrated via Liverpool aboard the Princeton bound for New York in 1852. [NARA]

GEOGHEGAN, EDWARD, a merchant in Philadelphia, America, will, 1741. [PWI]

GERRALD, JAMES, in Montserrat in 1677-1678. [TNA]

GERRALD, JOHN, in Montserrat in 1677-1678. [TNA]

GERRALD, MORRISH, in Montserrat in 1677-1678.
[TNA]

GERRALD, REDMOND, with one woman, in Montserrat in 1677-1678. [TNA]

GIBBONS, DAVID, in the parish of St John Capistar, St Kitts, on 28 January 1678. [TNA.COl.42]

GIBBS, DANIEL, a founder member of the Irish Charitable Society of Boston, Massachusetts, in 1736. [UJA.II.1.18]

GIBBS, VALENTINE, in Miramachi, New Brunswick, a letter, 1836. [PANB.MC1611]

GILBERT, Mrs ELIZA, [alias Lola Montez], born 1819 in Ireland, died in New York on 17 January 1861. [GM.ns2.10.349]

GILLIAN, JOHN, emigrated from Sligo on 25 April 1847 aboard the Aeolus of Greenock bound for New Brunswick, landed at St John on 31 May 1847.
[PANB.MC803]

GILLOON, ANDREW, emigrated from Sligo on 25 April 1847 aboard the Aeolus of Greenock bound for New Brunswick, landed at St John on 31 May 1847.
[PANB.MC803]

GILLOON, DENIS, emigrated from Sligo on 25 April 1847 aboard the Aeolus of Greenock bound for New Brunswick, landed at St John on 31 May 1847.
[PANB.MC803]

GILLOW, PATRICK, emigrated from Sligo on 25 April 1847 aboard the Aeolus of Greenock bound for New Brunswick, landed at St John on 31 May 1847.
[PANB.MC803]

GILLROY, JAMES, in Montserrat in 1677-1678. [TNA]

GILLROY, JOHN, in Montserrat in 1677-1678. [TNA]

GLANN, JOANNAS, an indentured servant who absconded in Pennsylvania on 17 June 1770. [PaGaz:19.6.1770]

GLASGANE, DENNIS, in Montserrat in 1677-1678. [TNA]

GLECHANE, MURLOW, in Montserrat in 1677-1678. [TNA]

GLEN, GEORGE, a founder member of the Irish Charitable Society of Boston, Massachusetts, in 1736. [UJA.II.1.18]

GLESSANE, JOHN, in Montserrat in 1677-1678. [TNA]

GONNE, WILLIAM HENRY, in Chatham, Ontario, letters, 1807. [PROI.M7158]

GOOLD, PEARCE, in Montserrat in 1677-1678. [TNA]

GOOLD, RICHARD, in Montserrat in 1677-1678. [TNA]

GORE, Captain JOHN, in America, a will, 1742. [PWI]

GORHIE, DONOUGH, born 1608, emigrated via London aboard the David, master John Hogg, bound for Virginia in September 1635. [TNA.E157.20]

GORMAN, CORNELIUS, in Montserrat in 1677-1678. [TNA]

GOULDSBURY, VALESIUS SKIPTON, eldest son of Valesius Gouldsbury in Longford, great grandson of I A Gouldsbury in Auchnogore, married Isobel Charlotte Perrott, third daughter of the late Edmund Thomas Perrott in Worcestershire, in Barbados on 8 September 1867. [GM.ns.2.17.647]

GOWNE, BRYAN, in Montserrat in 1677-1678. [TNA]

GRADY, JEFFREY, in Montserrat in 1677-1678. [TNA]

GRADY, JAMES, in the parish of Sandy Point, St Kitts on 7 February 1678. [TNA.COl.42]

GRADY, THOMAS, in Montserrat in 1677-1678. [TNA]

GRAHAM, or GRIMES, WILLIAM, an Irish pedlar in Pennsylvania in 1760s [Pa.Chronicle. 28.2.1768]

GRAHAM, ..., emigrated from Londonderry aboard the Ardent bound for Baltimore, Maryland, in 1803. [NEHGR.LX.163]

GREEN, PATRICK, in the parish of Sandy Point, St Kitts on 7 February 1678. [TNA.COl.42]

GREEN, ROBERT, son of John Green, born 1742, settled in Montreal, Quebec, died 1818. [Shankill gravestone, Belfast]

GREENE, WILLIAM, former Secretary of the Grand Canal Company of Dublin, died in Baltimore in 1805. [GM.75.677]

GREGG, JOHN, a farmer in Coleraine, County Londonderry, formerly in Virginia, will, 1747. [PWI]

GREY, CORNELIUS, in St Thomas, Middle Island, St Kitts on 7 February 1678. [TNA.COl.42]

GREY, ROBERT, emigrated from Sligo on 25 April 1847 aboard the Aeolus of Greenock bound for New Brunswick, landed at St John on 31 May 1847. [PANB.MC803]

GRIBBIN, THOMAS, emigrated to Canada in 1884, a letter. [PRONI.T2278.4]

GRIFFIN, ANTHONY, in Montserrat in 1677-1678. [TNA]

GRIFFEN, GEORGE, in Montserrat in 1677-1678. [TNA]

GRIFFEN, WILLIAM, in Montserrat in 1677-1678. [TNA]

GRIFFIN, WILLIAM, born 1751, a schoolmaster in Ireland, via London aboard the Baltimore bound for Baltimore as a redemptioner in 1775. [TNA.T47.9/11]

GRYNEN, JOHN, in Montserrat in 1677-1678. [TNA]

GUANE, EDMUND, in Montserrat in 1677-1678. [TNA]

GUANE, JAMES, in Montserrat in 1677-1678. [TNA]

GUANE, JOHN, in Montserrat in 1677-1678. [TNA]

HAGAN, BRIAN, died in Jamaica, administration, 1656 PCC. [TNA]

HAGARTY, CORNELIUS, born 1756, a gardener from Ireland, via London aboard the Baltimore bound for Baltimore as a redemptioner in 1775. [TNA.T47.9/11]

HAGGERTY, JOHN, from Ireland, an indentured servant aboard the Eleanor of Ireland, master Nicholas Reynolds, bound for Virginia in 1698. [LRO]

HALL, ALEXANDER, born 28 February 1751 in Tully, near Ramelton, County Donegal, late of Barbados, died in Bath on 27 March 1802. [Bath Abbey gravestone]

HALL, DAVID, born in Tully, County Donegal, around 1772, married Margaret Salter Alleyne in Barbados on 25 May 1811, a planter and merchant in Barbados, died in London on 4 September 1844, probate 14 September 1844, PCC. [TNA]

HALL, WILLIAM, President of the Irish Charitable Society of Boston, Massachusetts, in 1737. [UJA.II.1.18]

HALLERAN, DANIEL, in Montserrat in 1677-1678.
[TNA]

HALLERAN, FLORENCE, in Montserrat in 1677-1678.
[TNA]

HALLARAN, EDMOND, in Montserrat in 1677-1678.
[TNA]

HALLAS, TEIGE, in Montserrat in 1677-1678. [TNA]

HALY, JAMES, born 1766, a stationer and bookseller from Dublin, was naturalised in South Carolina in 1823. [NARA.M1183]

HALY, WILLIAM W., son of the late James Haly in Cork, died in Philadelphia on 26 December 1851. [GM.ns.37.312]

HAMILTON, WATSON, son of William and Sarah Hamilton in Belfast, died in San Francisco, California, in 1867. [Shankill gravestone, Belfast]

HAMMILL, DANIEL, born in Ireland, a schoolmaster in Charlotte County, New York, a Loyalist who moved to Annapolis Royal, Nova Scotia, by 1781.
[TNA.AO12.19.319]

HANNA, Mrs ELEANOR, born 1744, daughter of Mr McEntee in County Monaghan, widow of Thomas Hamilton, settled in USA in 1808, died in New York on 18 December 1856. [GM.ns.2.2.368]

HARAGIN, DANIEL, in the parish of Sandy Point, St Kitts on 7 February 1678. [TNA.COl.42]

HARBY, JOHN, in Montserrat in 1677-1678. [TNA]

HARDMAN, JOHN, emigrated from northern Ireland via Antigua to Pennsylvania before 1739. Sought there in 1738. [PA.Gaz.6.7.1738]

HARDMAN, JOHN, born 1743 in County Cavan, enlisted in the 22nd Regiment of Foot, a drummer, was wounded at the Siege of Louisbourg, served throughout the American Revolution, discharged in1787. [TNA.WO.121.1]

HARPER, JOHN, in Montserrat in 1677-1678. [TNA]

HARRA, OWEN, in Montserrat in 1677-1678. [TNA]

HARRIS, PETER, in Montserrat in 1677-1678. [TNA]

HARRIS, THOMAS, in Montserrat in 1677-1678. [TNA]

HART, JOAB, a merchant on Antigua, will, 1758. [PWI]

HART, JOHN, in Montserrat in 1677-1678. [TNA]

HART, PATRICK, emigrated from Sligo on 25 April 1847 aboard the Aeolus of Greenock bound for New Brunswick, landed at St John on 31 May 1847. [PANB.MC803]

HART, ROGER, a prisoner of war in St Domingo, will, 1788. [PWI]

HARVEY, WILLIAM, a merchant in Philadelphia, Pennsylvania, married Sally Brenan of Cole Alley, Meath Street, Dublin, in 1764, Both were Quakers. [FDJ.3843]

HATTON, THOMAS, a merchant in Market Street, Philadelphia, in 1729. [PaGaz.11.2.1729]

HAVAGHTY, PATRICK, emigrated from Sligo on 25 April 1847 aboard the Aeolus of Greenock bound for New Brunswick, landed at St John on 31 May 1847. [PANB.MC803]

HAWLEY, MARY ANN, born 6 February 1799 in Courtmasherry, County Cork, emigrated from Cork bound for Pockshaw on the Bay of Chaleur, New Brunswick, on 7 May 1822, settled in Newcastle, New Brunswick, later in Miramachi, New Brunswick. [PANB.MC1753]

HAYES, SAMUEL, from Dublin, an indentured servant bound from London for Antigua in 1755. [CLRO.ASP.8]

HAYNE, TEIGE, in Montserrat in 1677-1678. [TNA]

HAYS, NICHOLAS, a soldier stationed at Placentia, Newfoundland, in 1732. [TNA.CO194.24.109]

HEAK, WILLIAM, in Montserrat in 1677-1678. [TNA]

HEALY, JOHN, in St Thomas, Middle Island, St Kitts on 7 February 1678. [TNA.COI.42]

HEARLY, Sergeant RANDOLL, in Kayon Division, St Kitts on 7 February 1678. [TNA.COI.42]

HEAS, CORNELIUS, in Montserrat in 1677-1678. [TNA]

HEAS, JOHN, in Montserrat in 1677-1678. [TNA]

HEATHER, JAMES, settled in Canada, letters, 1833-1851. [PROI]

HELLEY, DAVID, born 1753, a laborer from Waterford, an indentured servant via London aboard the Peggy bound for Maryland in 1774. [TNA.T47.9/11]

HEMMING, WILLIAM, a merchant from Dublin, married Amey Hamilton in Barbados on 1 May 1755. [GM.25.236]

HENDERSON, JAMES, emigrated via Londonderry aboard the snow Frodsham, master James Aspinall, bound for Philadelphia in 1735, sought in 1740. [PaGaz.5.6.1740]

HENNESSY, CLAUDIUS, in Lower Canada, 1827. [NRS.GD45.3.534.]

HENNIS, DARBY, in the parish of Sandy Point, St Kitts on 7 February 1678. [TNA.COI.42]

HENRY, JOHN, in Richmond, Virginia, will, 1809. [PWI]

HENRY, ROBERT, fifth son of the late Joseph Henry in Dublin, married Ann Ramsay, second daughter of the late Nathaniel Thomas Ramsay of Barbados, in London on 10 November 1853. [GM.ns.41.185]

HERELY, DESMOND, in Montserrat in 1677-1678. [TNA]

HERELY, TEIGE, in Montserrat in 1677-1678. [TNA]

HEWITT, WILLIAM, Commissioner for the Ceded Islands, brother of the Lord Chancellor of Ireland, died in Barbados in 1781. [GM.51.489]

HEY, JOHN, in Montserrat in 1677-1678. [TNA]

HICKEY, MATHEW, a soldier stationed at Placentia, Newfoundland, in 1732. [TNA.CO194.24.109]

HICKEY, WILLIAM, a soldier stationed at Placentia, Newfoundland, in 1732. [TNA.CO194.24.109]

HIDE, JOHN, in Montserrat in 1677-1678. [TNA]

HIGGINS, CHARLES, in Montserrat in 1677-1678. [TNA]

HIGGINS, DAVID, with Philip Higgins aged 9, Benjamin Higgins age 6, Charles Higgins age 4, Mary Ann Higgins aged 2, and Nancy Higgins age 1, applied for a land grant in Bagot County, Lower Canada, in 1819. [LAC.RG1.L3.fos.66355-60]

HIGGIN, TEIGE, in Montserrat in 1677-1678. [TNA]

HILL, GEORGE, in Montserrat in 1677-1678. [TNA]

HILROY, NICHOLAS, in Montserrat in 1677-1678. [TNA]

HODGE, FRANCIS, and his wife and family, from Ballibay, County Monaghan, emigrated to America in 1827, settled in Delhi, Delaware County, New York.

HODGES, RICHARD, in Montserrat in 1677-1678. [TNA]

HOGAN, EDMOND, in Montserrat in 1677-1678. [TNA]

HOGAN, MATTHEW, in the parish of Sandy Point, St Kitts on 7 February 1678. [TNA.COl. 42]

HOGAN, NICHOLAS, applied for a land grant in Bagot County, Lower Canada in 1819. [LAC.RG1.L3.ff 66355-60]

HOKINS, CLEMENT, in Montserrat in 1677-1678. [TNA]

HOKINS, CLEMENT, jr, with a woman and children, in Montserrat in 1677-1678. [TNA]

HOLLAND, JOHN, born 1743 in Ireland, a tailor, was recruited in Boston, Massachusetts, in 1758 by Captain Cosnan of the 45th Regiment of Foot. [NRS.GD45.2.24.4B]

HOLMES, HUGH, a merchant in Antigua, will, 1762. [PWI]

HOLMES, JOHN, jr., from Belfast, married Miss Daniell, only daughter of Thomas Daniell, the Attorney General of Dominica, in Snesham, Norfolk, on 1 April 1802. [GM.72.373]

HOLT, JOHN, from Dublin, a mariner in Philadelphia, will, 1750. [PWI]

HOPKINS, Reverend JOHN HENRY, born 1792 in Dublin, Bishop of Vermont, died at Rock Point, Vermont, on 9 January 1868. [GM.ns.3.5.390]

HOPPER, ANTHONY, born 1756 in Ireland, a painter, from London aboard the Neptune bound for Maryland in 1775. [TNA.T47.9/11]

HORANE, JOHN, in Montserrat in 1677-1678. [TNA]

HORAN, WILLIAM, sr. in St Thomas, Middle Island, St Kitts on 7 February 1678. [TNA.COI. 42]

HORAN, WILLIAM, jr. in St Thomas, Middle Island, St Kitts on 7 February 1678. [TNA.COI. 42]

HORE, Lieutenant E G, son of the late Captain Hore of the Royal Navy, of Pole Hore, Wexford, married Maria Reid, second daughter of Lieutenant Colonel Reid, Governor of the Windward Islands, in Barbados on 17 June 1847. [GM.ns28.312]

HORNBY, WILLIAM, in South Carolina, will, 1788. [PWI]

HOSSEY, OWEN, in Montserrat in 1677-1678. [TNA]

HUDSHELL, JOHN, in Montserrat in 1677-1678. [TNA]

IRISH EMIGRANTS IN NORTH AMERICA, Volume 9

HUGHES, EDWARD, possibly from Newry, in Summit, Cambria County, Pennsylvania, a letter, 1852. [PANB.MC2618]

HUGHES, LAWRENCE, in Fredericton, New Brunswick, a letter, 1837, possibly from Newry. [PANB.MC2618]

HUGHES, PATRICK, possibly from Newry, in Milltown, St Stephen, New Brunswick, a letter, 1851. [PANB.MC2618]

HUKEY, ROBERT, in Montserrat in 1677-1678. [TNA]

HUMPHREY, JAMES, from Croagh, settled in Upper Canada in 1824. [PRONI.T3534.2]

HUMPHREYS, THOMAS, a planter in Kingston, Jamaica, 1773, [see John Humphreys' will, 1775, in Dublin Register of Deeds]

HUNTER, JOSEPH, in Dalhousie, New Brunswick, letters, 1841-1843. [NLI.20329; 20340]

HUNTER, THOMAS, formerly of Birr, King's County, now of Anson, North Carolina, will, 1771. [PWI]

HUPTOW, MURTOW in St Thomas, Middle Island, St Kitts on 7 February 1678. [TNA.COI.42]

HURLEY, DENNIS, settled in Carson City, Nevada, a letter dated 1892. [CA.U170.18]

HYDEN, GREGORY, in Montserrat in 1677-1678. [TNA]

HYNDMAN, THOMAS, from Antigua, died at Glen Oak, County Antrim on 3 September 1815. [GM.85.376]IRWIN, JOHN R., an Ensign in the West Indies, a journal from 1808 to 1813. [PRONI.DOD.1515.1]

48

IRWIN, ALEXANDER BURROWES, late of the 32nd Regiment, a planter in St Vincent, died on 22 July 1806. [St Vincent gravestone]

ISAAC, WILLIAM, born 1700 in County Cavan, a weaver, a sergeant of the 35th Foot at Fort Edward in 1757. [TNA.WO.116.5.20]

IVORY, THOMAS, a soldier stationed at Placentia, Newfoundland, in 1732. [TNA.CO194.24.109]

JAMES, JOHN, in Montserrat in 1677-1678. [TNA]

JANEY, JOHN, in Montserrat in 1677-1678. [TNA]

JOHN, OWEN, emigrated from Sligo on 25 April 1847 aboard the Aeolus of Greenock bound for New Brunswick, landed at St John on 31 May 1847. [PANB.MC803]

JOHNSTON, ROBERT, Governor of South Carolina, will, 1800. [PWI]

JOLLY, CONSTAN, in Montserrat in 1677-1678. [TNA]

JONES, VALENTINE, born 1729, son of Valentine Jones [1711-1805], a merchant in Barbados, returned to Ireland in 1783, a merchant in Belfast, died in Portpatrick in 1808.

JOYCE, ROBERT, an indentured servant, from Tane, County Galway, Ireland, aboard the Elisabeth and Ann, master William Benn, bound for Montserrat in March 1699. [LRO]

JOYCE, WILLIAM, from Cork, in Newfoundland, 1770, husband of Catherine Slattery. [FMC.23.7.1770]

JOHNSON, CORNELIUS, in Halfwaytree Division, St Kitts on 7 February 1678. [TNA.COI.42]

JOHNSON, JOB, a schoolmaster in Oxford township, Pennsylvania, a letter, 1767. [PRONI.T3700.1]

JOHNSON, WILLIAM, a schoolmaster in Charleston, South Carolina, possibly from Dungannon, died before 1769. [PRONI.D1044.176]

JOHNSTON, ADAM, emigrated from Sligo on 25 April 1847 aboard the Aeolus of Greenock bound for New Brunswick, landed at St John on 31 May 1847. [PANB.MC803]

JOHNSTON, EDWARD, emigrated from Sligo on 25 April 1847 aboard the Aeolus of Greenock bound for New Brunswick, landed at St John on 31 May 1847. [PANB.MC803]

JOHNSTON, WILLIAM, a farmer in Saintfield, County Down, bound for America in 1772. [BNL:1.9.1773]

JOHNSTON, WILLIAM, emigrated from Sligo on 25 April 1847 aboard the Aeolus of Greenock bound for New Brunswick, landed at St John on 31 May 1847. [PANB.MC803]

JONES, CHARLES, emigrated from Sligo on 25 April 1847 aboard the Aeolus of Greenock bound for New Brunswick, landed at St John on 31 May 1847. [PANB.MC803]

KAVENAUGH, ROBERT, from Muckalee, County Kilkenny, emigrated to Canada in 1847. [Globe and Mail: 19.2.1848]

KAVENAUGH, THOMAS, from Muckalee, County Kilkenny, emigrated to Canada in 1847. [Globe and Mail: 19.2.1848]

IRISH EMIGRANTS IN NORTH AMERICA, Volume 9

KEAGH, MICHAEL, in Montserrat in 1677-1678. [TNA]

KEANE, MICHAEL, born 1739, died in Antigua on 11 June 1796. [St Michael's Cathedral, Antigua]

KEARNEY, JAMES, a soldier of the 2nd Battalion of the 84th Regiment, commanded by Major John Small, aboard the frigate Raleigh, Captain Gambier, from New York bound for Charleston, South Carolina, in 1780. [NRS.GD174.2405]

KEEFE, THOMAS, a merchant at Harbour Grace, Newfoundland, 1780. [W.381]

KEENE, CORNELIUS, in Montserrat in 1677-1678. [TNA]

KEEN, JANE, a widow in Carolina, will, 1792. [PWI]

KEENE, WILLIAM, sr., in Kayon Division, St Kitts on 7 February 1678. [TNA.COI.42]

KEENE, WILLIAM, jr, in Kayon Division, St Kitts on 7 February 1678. [TNA.COI.42]

KELLY, ANDREW, in Montserrat in 1677-1678. [TNA]

KELLY, BRIAN, born 1615, emigrated via London aboard the Safety, mater John Graunt, bound for Virginia in August 1635. [TNA.E157.20]

KELLY, BRYAN, in Nevis, 1677-1678. [TNA]

KELLY, DANIEL, in the parish of Sandy Point, St Kitts on 7 February 1678. [TNA.COI.42]

KELLY, DENNIS, in the parish of Sandy Point, St Kitts on 7 February 1678. [TNA.COI.42]

KELLY, DENIS, late of Jamaica, now in Lisduffe, County Galway, will, 1757. [PWI]

KELLY, JOHN, in Montserrat in 1677-1678. [TNA]

KELLY, JOHN, in St Thomas, Middle Island, St Kitts on 7 February 1678. [TNA.COI.42]

KELLY, JOHN, with one woman and three children, in Montserrat in 1677-1678. [TNA]

KELLY, JOHN, born 1732, a cooper from Armagh, an indentured servant bound via London for Georgia in June 1752. [CLRO.ASP.6]

KELLY, MATHEW, a soldier stationed at Placentia, Newfoundland, in 1732. [TNA.CO194.24.109]

KELLY, PETER, a fisherman from Cork, an indentured servant bound via Bristol for Virginia in 1655. [BRO]

KELLY, TEIGE, in Montserrat in 1677-1678. [TNA]

KELLY, THOMAS, in Montserrat in 1677-1678. [TNA]

KELLY, WALTER, wife Mary, and a son, in Nevis, 1677-1678. [TNA]

KELSEY, HENRY, a tailor in Buenos Ayres, Spanish Indies, will, 1749. [PWI]

KENNEDY, JOHN, a Sergeant, stationed at Placentia, Newfoundland, in 1732. [TNA.CO194.24.109]

KENNEDY, PATRICK, in Montserrat in 1677-1678. [TNA]

KENNEDY, VALENTINE, in Savanna, Georgia, a letter, 1835. [PANB.MC1729; MS1.D.01]

KENNY, JAMES, in Montserrat in 1677-1678. [TNA]

KEOGH, MYLES WALTER, [1840-1876], an army officer in America, letters, 1861-1869, to his brother Thomas Keogh in Carlow, Ireland. [NLI.ms3885]

KERBY, THOMAS NORBURY, Commander-in-Chief of Antigua and Montserrat, died in Antigua during November 1819. [F.J.4.2.1820]

KILLMURY, DANIEL, in Montserrat in 1677-1678. [TNA]

KING, ELIZABETH, daughter of Abraham King in Dublin, an indentured servant aboard the Eleanor of Ireland, master Nicholas Reynolds, bound for Virginia in 1698. [LRO]

KING, GILBERT, an Ensign of the British Army in Canada and New York, a notebook, 1761-1768. [NLI.MS3240]

KING, HUGH, in Montserrat in 1677-1678. [TNA]

KNOWLES, Lieutenant, WILLIAM, on Montserrat, 1677. [TNA]

KNOWLES, WILLIAM, in Montserrat in 1677-1678. [TNA]

KNOX, ANDREW, a founder member of the Irish Charitable Society of Boston, Massachusetts, in 1736. [UJA.II.1.18]

KYON, CORNELIUS, in Montserrat in 1677-1678. [TNA]

LACKEY, JANE, from Carrickfergus, Ireland, aboard the Experiment of Liverpool, master Cavaleiro Christian, bound for America in August 1699. [LRO]

LADD, CORNELIUS, sr., in Kayon Division, St Kitts on 7 February 1678. [TNA.COI.42]

LADD, CORNELIUS, jr, in Kayon Division, St Kitts on 7 February 1678. [TNA.COI.42]

LAIRD, SAMUEL, son of James Laird in Desmartin, County Londonderry, graduated MA from Glasgow University in 1751, a minister emigrated to North Carolina in 1755, [EMA.40][FPA.304/327][MAGU.319]

LALOR, WILLIAM, a farmer in Wisconsin, letters, 1843-1884. [NLI.MS8567]

LAMB, THOMAS, formerly a merchant in Jamaica, now in London, will, 1701. [PWI]

LAMBERT, PATRICK, born in Gurtinminogue, Kildavin, County Wexford, 1754, a priest in Newfoundland, later a Bishop, died 1816.

LANDERGAN, JAMES, a planter at Cupids, Newfoundland, in 1820. [TNA.CO194.64.248-258]

LANE, DARBY, in Montserrat in 1677-1678. [TNA]

LATIMER, RICHARD, from Kingston, Jamaica, died in Crumlin, Ireland, on 30 October 1813. [GM.83.622]

LEAHA, WILLIAM, in the parish of Sandy Point, St Kitts on 7 February 1678. [TNA.COI.42]

LEAHY, Sergeant WILLIAM, , in Montserrat in 1677-1678. [TNA]

LEARY, CORNELIUS, in Montserrat in 1677-1678. [TNA]

LEE, PETER, born 1660 in Dublin, lived in England, fought n Flanders, died in Antigua on 8 October 1704. [St John's Cathedral, Antigua]

LEAUE, TEGO, from Cork, Ireland, aged 30, from emigrated via Plymouth aboard the Robert Bonaventure bound for St Kitts in February 1633. [TNA]

LEITCH, JOHN, in Montserrat in 1677-1678. [TNA]

LEMMON, RICHARD, in Baltimore, America, will, 1797. [PWI]

LERNANE, DERMOND, in Montserrat in 1677-1678. [TNA]

LEWIS, HENRY, in Montserrat in 1677-1678. [TNA]

LIFORD, JOHN, a clerk in Sherby Hundred, Virginia, will, 1632. [PWI]

LINDSAY, DAVID, from Newry, a mariner settled in New Hanover County, North Carolina, will subscribed in 1754. [New Hanover County Wills]

LINDSAY, DAVID, from Rathfriland, County Down, a soldier in Barbados, letters, 1804-1808. [PRONI.DOD.687]

LINDSAY, JOHN, from Ballymena, County Antrim, an indentured servant, bound from Liverpool aboard the Elizabeth and Ann, for Montserrat in 1700. [LRO]

LINDSAY, WILLIAM, in Antigua, will, 1763. [PWI]

LITTLE, JAMES, born 1759 in Wexford, a husbandman, from London aboard the Bland bound for Virginia in 1775. [TNA.T47.9/11]

LITTLE, JOHN, a founder member of the Irish
Charitable Society of Boston, Massachusetts, in 1736.
[UJA.II.1.18]

LITTLE, PHILIP FRANCIS, a judge in Newfoundland,
married Mary Jane Holdright, daughter of Edward
Holdright of Monkstown, in Kingstown, Dublin, on 4
May 1864. [GM.ns.2.16.795]

LOCKE, RICHARD, a storekeeper in Bonafacio,
Florida, son of John Locke in Dublin, letters 1880-1890.
[NLI]

LONDREGAN. THOMAS, born 1752, a Roman Catholic
priest, arrived in Placentia, Newfoundland, in 1785, died
in Fogo in 1787.

LONG, JOHN, in Montserrat in 1677-1678. [TNA]

LONG, TEIGE, in Montserrat in 1677-1678. [TNA]

LONG, WILLIAM, in St Thomas, Middle Island, St Kitts
on 7 February 1678. [TNA.COI.42]

LORRY, DERMOND, in Montserrat in 1677-1678. [TNA]

LOUGHLAN, JAMES, in Montserrat in 1677-1678.
[TNA]

LOVE, SAMUEL, and his wife Sarah, from
Baillieborough, emigrated to America in 1801, settled in
Delhi, Delaware County, New York.

LOVETT, THOMAS, from Belfast and Virginia, died at
sea aboard HMS Falkland, probate, 1709, PCC. [TNA]

LOY, RICHARD, in Montserrat in 1677-1678. [TNA]

LUBY, THOMAS CLARKE, [1821-1901], in Newark,
New Jersey, letters. [NLI.MS331]

LUCAS, ROBERT, born 1723 in Armagh, a soldier of the 27th Regiment of Foot, fought in New York around 1759 during the French and Indian Wars. [TNA.WO.120.4]

LUKE, CAMPBELL, son of James and Catherine Luke in Belfast, died in Philadelphia, Pennsylvania, in 1820. [New Burying Ground gravestone, Belfast]

LUKE, WILLIAM, son of James and Catherine Luke in Belfast, died in New York in 1837. [New Burying Ground gravestone, Belfast]

LYNCH, ANDREW, in Montserrat in 1677-1678. [TNA]

LYNCH, ANTHONY, in St Kitts, probate, 1757, PCC. [TNA]

LYNCH, ANTHONY, died 18 July 1766 in Barbados. [St Michael's Cathedral burial register]

LYNCH, CHRISTOPHER, in Montserrat in 1677-1678. [TNA]

LYNCH, DISNEY, deserted the 60th Regiment in New York, later court martialled at Fort George, NY, in 1757. [TNA.WO.71.66]

LYNCH, FRANCIS, in Montserrat in 1677-1678. [TNA]

LYNCH, HELLENOR, from Antigua, died in Barbados on 6 May 1682. [St Michael's Cathedral, Barbados parish register]

LINCH, JOHN, in Montserrat in 1677-1678. [TNA]

LINCH, MARCUS, in Montserrat in 1677-1678. [TNA]

LYNCH, MICHAEL, in Montserrat in 1677-1678. [TNA]

LYNCH, PEARE, in Montserrat in 1677-1678. [TNA]

LYNCH, PHILIP, late of the parish of St Katherine's, Jamaica, late in the parish of St James, Westminster, London, will refers to his uncle John Ormsby in Dublin, his nephew Philip Athy, son of his sister Margaret Athy, nephew John Athy, brother in law Edmond Athy, friends Edmond Kelly and Andrew Archdecken; witnesses Revered Samuel Hawes in Westminster, William Stephens a brazier in Westminster and his wife Mary, William Dick and Thomas Londry, probate 9 May 1717. [DRD]

LYNCH, THOMAS, in Montserrat in 1677-1678. [TNA]

LYON, BENJAMIN, in St Catherine's, Jamaica, will, 1781. [PWI]

MCALEXANDER, ALEXANDER, a tory who surrendered, taken to Dublin, to be transported beyond the sea, 19 October 1669. [CSPI.1669]

MCALEXANDER, TOALBOY, a tory who surrendered, taken to Dublin, to be transported beyond the sea, 19 October 1669. [CSPI.1669]

MCBRIAN, DENNIS, born 1617, emigrated via London aboard the Alexander, Captain Burche, bound for Barbados in May 1635. [TNA. E157.20]

MCCARTY, JOHN, in Lower Canada, 1827. [NRS.GD45.3.534.8]

MCATYER, JOHN, in Albany, New York, a letter, 1766. [PRONI.D530.22]

MCCALL, ..., brother of John McCall in Lurgan, emigrated to Antigua before 1713. [TCD.750.1475]

MCCARTIE, CHARLES, born 1608, emigrated via London aboard the Plain Jane, master Richard Buckam, bound for Virginia in May 1635. [TNA.E157.20]

MCCARTIE, OWEN, born 1617, emigrated via London aboard the Plain Jane, master Richard Buckam, bound for Virginia in May 1635. [TNA.E157.20]

MCCARTY, TEIGE, in Montserrat in 1677-1678. [TNA]

MCCAUL, Reverend JOHN, from Dublin, Principal of Upper Canada College, married Emily Jones, daughter of Justice Jones, in Toronto in 1839. [GM.ns13.201]

MCCAUSLAND, CAROLINE, second daughter of Oliver McCausland in Letterkenny, died in Union Island, St Vincent, on 8 June 1798. [GM.68.627]

MCCLALAND, SARAH, from Nottingham, daughter of the late Joseph McClaland in Kingston, Jamaica, married John Mayne of Houndsgate, Nottingham, in Dublin on 16 June 1798. [GM.68.624]

MCCLELLAND, ..., emigrated via Cork aboard the Kangaroo bound for New York in 1860. [PRONI.T3234.102]

MCCLENAHAN, DAVID, a merchant in Princess Ann County, Virginia, born 1697, died in Barbados on 30 October 1735, son of Nathaniel McClenahan a merchant in Virginia and his wife Elizabeth McClenahan. [St Michael's Cathedral gravestone, Barbados]

MCCOLGAN, GRIZZY, from Belfast, settled in Hanover township, Lancaster County, Pennsylvania, before 1776. [Londonderry Journal: 1.6.1784]

MCCONNELL, ALEXANDER, died 1729 in Chester County, Pennsylvania. [Chester County inventories 348]

MCCONNELL, GILBERT, and his wife Jane [who died on 9 August 1783], parents of John [died 20 September 1778], Gilbert [died August 1783], and Lane [died August 1783] [St John's Cathedral, Antigua]

MCCONNELL, JOHN, born 1754 in Belfast, an indentured servant who absconded in Pennsylvania in 1774. [PaGaz:9.2.1774]

MCCONRY, JOHN, born 1607, emigrated via London aboard the Alexander bound for Barbados in May 1635. [TNA.E157.20]

MCCORMACK, JAMES, born on 6 August 1751, settled in New Windsor, New York, died on 11 November 1865, in Newburgh, New York. [GM.ns3.1.283]

MACCOWDIN, WILLIAM, born 1616, emigrated via London aboard the Peter Bonaventure, master Thomas Harman, bound for Barbados or St Kitts in April 1635. [TNA.E157.20]

MCCULLOCH, ALEXANDER, of Ballycopeland, County Down, bound for America in 1718. [NRS.GD10.1421.I.46]

MCCULLOCH, JOHN, born 1716 in northern Ireland, Provincial officer under Rogers, and Stores Commissary at Oswego in 1756, died in London on 27 December 1793. [GM.ns64.89]

MCCULLOUGH, JOHN, probably from Ballymena, emigrated to Philadelphia, Pennsylvania, in 1772. [BNL:5.5.1772]

MCCULLOUGH, ..., emigrated from Londonderry aboard the Ardent bound for Baltimore, Maryland, in 1803. [NEHGR.LX.163]

MCCUNN, JOHN, born 1753 in Ireland, a cabinet-maker, from London aboard the Pennsylvania Packet bound for Philadelphia in 1775. [TNA.T47.9/11]

MCCURDY, ARCHIBALD, a pedler in Lancaster County, Pennsylvania, in 1751. [PaGaz.31.10.1751]

MCDANIEL, ALEXANDER, in Montserrat in 1677-1678. [TNA]

MCDANIEL, BRYAN, a merchant at Black River on the Mosquito Shore in America, deed, 1772. [NRS.GD77.165]

MCDERMOT, CATHERINE, emigrated aboard the Needham, Captain Cheevers, bound for Newcastle, Delaware, in 1773. [PaJournal:8.9.1773]

MCDONALD, TERENCE, a Roman Catholic priest, died 10 November 1775, probate St Jan, Danish West Indies. [RAK. 1758-1775.222-225]

MCDONNELL, ART, a tory who surrendered, taken to Dublin, to be transported beyond the sea, 19 October 1669. [CSPI.1669]

MCDONNELL, FERDORROUGH, a tory who surrendered, taken to Dublin, to be transported beyond the sea, 19 October 1669. [CSPI.1669]

MCDONNELL, GILESPRIG, a tory who surrendered, taken to Dublin, to be transported beyond the sea, 19 October 1669. [CSPI.1669]

MCDONNELL, JOHN, possibly from Dungannon, settled in Wilmington, North Carolina, by 1771, a letter. [PRONI.D1044.294]

MCDONNELL, OWEN DUFF, a tory who surrendered, taken to Dublin, to be transported beyond the sea, 19 October 1669. [CSPI.1669]

MCDONNELL, RANDALL, a tory who surrendered, taken to Dublin, to be transported beyond the sea, 19 October 1669. [CSPI.1669]

MCDONNELL, RANDALL, late of Barbados, now a merchant in Dublin, will, 1743. [PWI]

MCDONNELL, RORY, a tory who surrendered, taken to Dublin, to be transported beyond the sea, 19 October 1669. [CSPI.1669]

MCDONELL, RANDALL, late a merchant in Barbados, now in Dublin, will, 1743. [PWI]

MCDONNELL, SORLEY, a tory who surrendered, taken to Dublin, to be transported beyond the sea, 19 October 1669. [CSPI.1669]

MCDONNELL, TERLAGH, a tory who surrendered, taken to Dublin, to be transported beyond the sea, 19 October 1669. [CSPI.1669]

MCDONELL, Miss, daughter of the late Charles McDonell in Newhall, County Clare, married Charles Hamilton from Tobago, on 23 October 1799. [GM.69.1192]

MCDONOUGH, HENRY, in Montserrat in 1677-1678. [TNA]

MCDONAGH, JOHN, a planter, died 1 April 1745, husband of Susanna ……, probate St Croix, Danish West Indies, 1741-1748, fo.253. [RAK]

MCDONOUGH, MATTHEW, died 24 April 1762, probate Frederickstad, Danish West Indies, 1760-1775, Fos.10-39. [RAK]

MCDOWELL, JOHN, from Belfast, minister of St Philips, Brunswick, New Hanover County, North Carolina, husband of Sarah Thompson {?}, died 1765. [New Hanover County Wills]

MCEVERS, JOHN, emigrated to New York in 1716, died in 1751; a merchant in New York, a letter, 1734. [PRONI.D354.684]

MCFALL, DANIEL, a founder member of the Irish Charitable Society of Boston, Massachusetts, in 1736. [UJA.II.1.18]

MCFARRAN, JOHN, Solicitor General in the Caribee Islands, will, 1790. [PWI]

MCGAREL, CHARLES, born 1788 in Larne, emigrated to Demerara, a merchant in Stabroek later called Georgetown by 1808. [PRONI.T528.38]

MCGAWYN, BRIAN, emigrated via London aboard the Transport of London, master Edward Walker, bound for Virginia in July 1635. [TNA.E157.20]

MCGEE, REBECCA, died in St Jan, Danish West Indies, on 18 December 1827, probate, St Jan, 1826-1836, fos. 30-43.

MCGEE, THOMAS D'ARCY, born 1823 in Carlingford, died in Ottawa in 1868. [GM.ns.3.5.690]

MCGILCOAN, JAMES DUFF, a tory who surrendered, taken to Dublin, to be transported beyond the sea, 19 October 1669. [CSPI.1669]

MCGAREL, CHARLES, born in Larne 1788, a merchant planter and slave owner in the West Indies and Guyana, died 1876 in London. [PRONI.T528.38]

MCGEE, THOMAS D'ARCY, born 1823 in Carlingford, died in Ottawa in 1868. [GM.ns3/5.690]

MCGILL, MARY, emigrated from Londonderry aboard the Rose, master Joseph Curry, bound for Baltimore, Maryland, in 1775, an indentured servant in Lancaster County, Pennsylvania, absconded in 1776. [PaGaz.8.1776]

MCGILL, NEALE, a tory who surrendered, taken to Dublin, to be transported beyond the sea, 19 October 1669. [CSPI.1669]

MCGILLIGAN, BRIAN, a tory who surrendered, taken to Dublin, to be transported beyond the sea, 19 October 1669. [CSPI.1669]

MCGINITY, THOMAS, emigrated to New York in 1847, a letter. [PRONI.T3539.1]

MAGRA, JOHN, in Montserrat in 1677-1678. [TNA]

MAGRA, WILLIAM, a soldier stationed at Placentia, Newfoundland, in 1732. [TNA.CO194.24.109]

MAGRATH, JAMES, born 1767, educated at Trinity College, Dublin, a minister of the Church of Ireland, formerly of Shankhill and Castlerea, emigrated, with his wife, 5 children and a nephew, to Upper Canada in 1827, settled in Erindale on the Credit River, died on 14 June 1851. [PRONI.Mic205/1][GM.ns.36.327]

MCGRATH, TERENCE, a soldier of the 2nd Battalion of the 84th Regiment, commanded by Major John Small, aboard the frigate Raleigh, Captain Gambier, from New York bound for Charleston, South Carolina, in 1780. [NRS.GD174.2405]

MAGRA, THURLOGH, in Montserrat in 1677-1678. [TNA]

MCGRATH, Reverend Dr, born in Dublin, late of St Mark's in Liverpool, Rector of Trelawney in Jamaica, died on 14 June 1852. [GM.ns38.320]

MCGUYER, ROGER, in Montserrat in 1677-1678. [TNA]

MCILVEEN, AGNES, born 1868, daughter of Agnes Clark, died in East Norwalk, Oxen., USA, on 2 July 1898. [Shankill MI, Belfast.]

MCKINNEY, ALEXANDER, a merchant in Nevis and St Kitts in 1661, agent for George McCartney a merchant in Belfast. [PRONI.MCI19.1]

MACKINTOSH, JOHN and MARGARET, in Portland, St John, New Brunswick, 1851. [PANB.MC1132]

MACINTYRE, NEIL, President of the Irish Charitable Society of Boston, Massachusetts, in 1743. [UJA.II.1.18]

MACKAY, JAMES, a mariner from Londonderry, died in Antigua, probate, 1693, PCC. [TNA]

MCKEE, WILLIAM, emigrated aboard the Needham, Captain Cheevers, bound for Newcastle, Delaware, in 1773. [PaJournal:8.9.1773]

MCKEE, ..., emigrated from Londonderry aboard the Ardent bound for Baltimore, Maryland, in 1803.
[NEHGR.LX.163]

MCKELMORE, ROBERT, died in Pennsylvania in 1734. [Lancaster County Historical Society, inventories 92, folder 2]

MCKILLOP, CHARLES, from Belfast, emigrated aboard the Earl of Holderness, master William Blair, bound for Philadelphia, Pennsylvania, in 1752. [Lancaster County History Society: Hanover Town Tax List]

MCKINNEY, WILLIAM, from Sentry Hill, Carmoney, County Antrim, emigrated via Cork aboard the Kangaroo bound for New York in 1860.
[PRONI.T3234.102]

MCKINSTRY, HENRY, from the north of Ireland, settled in St Kitts, British West Indies, by 1731.
[PRONI.D162.24]

MCKINSTRY, HENRIETTA, wife of Colonel McKinstry of the 17th Regiment, sister of Charles W O'Hara in County Sligo, died in Toronto on 8 February 1867.
[GM.ns3.3.541]

MCLAUGHLIN, JOHN, emigrated from Sligo on 25 April 1847 aboard the Aeolus of Greenock bound for New Brunswick, landed at St John on 31 May 1847.
[PANB.MC803]

MACLEY, THOMAS, in Tullywhisker, Urney parish, County Tyrone, bound for America in 1769.
[PRONI.D623.A37.159]

MACLOUGHLAN, OWEN, in Montserrat in 1677-1678.
[TNA]

MCMAHON, Reverend FRANCIS, born 1759, Rector of St Paul's, Grenada from 1784 to 1784, and Rector of St John and St Mathew, Grenada, from 1795, died 22 November 1827. [Grenada gravestone]

MCMANUS, REDMOND, in Montserrat in 1677-1678. [TNA]

MCMIN, JOSEPH, born 1722, a weaver, with his wife Mary, born 1732, and child, emigrated from Belfast aboard the brig Polly bound for Philadelphia, Pennsylvania, in 1771. [PaGaz:6.2.1772]

MCMURRAY, JAMES, in Fredericktown, USA, letters, 1786, 1804. [PRONI.D4031.F19.1]

MACNAMARA, DENNIS, in Montserrat in 1677-1678. [TNA]

MCNAMAROE, DANIEL, in the parish of Sandy Point, St Kitts on 7 February 1678. [TNA.COI.42]

MCNEIL, CHARLES, a shoemaker, emigrated from Londonderry aboard the Jupiter, Captain Ewing, bound for Pennsylvania, an indentured servant who absconded in 1773. [PaGaz: 10.11.1773]

MCNEMARA, Mrs MARY, born 1723, wife of Michael McNemara MD, died in Barbados on 8 February 1757. [St Michael's Cathedral MI, Barbados]

MCNEVIN, Dr WILLIAM JAMES, born 1763, 'Irish rebel and companion of Emmett', died in New York in 1841. [GM.ms16.447]

MCNUFF, MORTON, in Montserrat in 1677-1678. [TNA]

MCQUADE, REDMOND, a tory who surrendered, taken to Dublin, to be transported beyond the sea, 19 October 1669. [CSPI.1669]

MCQUADE, RORY, a tory who surrendered, taken to Dublin, to be transported beyond the sea, 19 October 1669. [CSPI.1669]

MACQUIRE, PETER, born 1758, a labourer from Ireland, via Bristol aboard the Fortune bound for Maryland as an indentured servant in 1775. [TNA.T47.9/11]

MCREGANE, MILES, in Montserrat in 1677-1678. [TNA]

MCTEIGE, REMOND, in Montserrat in 1677-1678. [TNA]

MCTREVER, SOLOMON, a tory who surrendered, taken to Dublin, to be transported beyond the sea, 19 October 1669. [CSPI.1669]

MACHUM, ALEXANDER, born 1796 in County Derry, a linen weaver, emigrated from Londonderry aboard the Aurora bound for St John, New Brunswick, died 1868, father of Alexander, Martha, Ann, John, James, Samuel, and Mary Jane. [PANB.MC1847]

MADDEN, Mrs HELEN MARTHA, born 1818, widow of Charles Madden in Kilkenny, died in London, Ontario, on 28 November 1862. [GM.ns.2714.255]

MADAN, JANE, in St Kitts, probate, 1791, PCC. [TNA]

MAGRATH, Reverend JAMES, born 1766, educated at Trinity College in Dublin, late in Shankhill and Castlerea, Rector of Toronto, died in Erindale, Ontario, on 14 June 1851. [GM.ns36.327]

MADANE, MARCUS, in Montserrat in 1677-1678. [TNA]

MADDIN, DONOUGH, in Montserrat in 1677-1678. [TNA]

MAHANY, DENNIS, born 1748, a sailor from Ireland, , via London aboard the Baltimore bound for Baltimore as a redemptioner in 1775. [TNA.T47.9/11]

MAHON, MICHAEL, of the Kingdom of Ireland, and his wife Margaret ..., died 16..., parents of James Mahon. [St Michael's Cathedral MI, Barbados]

MAHONE, WILLIAM, in Montserrat in 1677-1678. [TNA]

MAHONEY, CORNELIUS, in Montserrat in 1677-1678. [TNA]

MAHONEY, DENNIS, in Montserrat in 1677-1678. [TNA]

MAHONEY, GEORGE, in St Kitts, probate, 1799, PCC. [TNA]

MAHONEY, GLASNEY, in Montserrat in 1677-1678. [TNA]

MAHONEY, JEREMIAH, died 2 April 1746, probate, St Croix, 1741-1748, fo.350. [RAK]

MAHONEY, JOHN, in Montserrat in 1677-1678. [TNA]

MAHONEY, TEIGE, in Montserrat in 1677-1678. [TNA]

MAHONEY, WILLIAM, in Montserrat in 1677-1678. [TNA]

MAHOOD, SARAH, emigrated from Newry aboard the Newry's Assistance bound for Philadelphia, Pennsylvania, landed there in January 1772.

MAHOOK, RICHARD, in Montserrat in 1677-1678.
[TNA]

MAIDEN, MARCUS, jr., in Montserrat in 1677-1678.
[TNA]

MAKAR, JAMES, born 1750 in Ireland, a husbandman from London aboard the Maryland Planter bound for Maryland in 1775. [TNA.T47.9/11]

MAKE, PETER, in Montserrat in 1677-1678. [TNA]

MALLOW, MORGAN, in Montserrat in 1677-1678.
[TNA]

MALLY, DERMOND, in Montserrat in 1677-1678. [TNA]

MALLY, JOHN, in Montserrat in 1677-1678. [TNA]

MANSFIELD, MORRIS, in Montserrat in 1677-1678.
[TNA]

MANSFIELD, OWEN, in Iroquois County, Illinois, letters, 1874-1875 to his brother George Patrick Lattin Mansfield, [1820-1889], of Morristown Lattin, County Kildare. [NLI.Mansfield Letters]

MANSFIELD, Ensign THOMAS, in Montserrat in 1677-1678. [TNA]

MANSFIELD, THOMAS, jr., in Montserrat in 1677-1678.
[TNA]

MANSLANE, DARBY, in Montserrat in 1677-1678.
[TNA]

MARLYN, DENNIS, in Montserrat in 1677-1678. [TNA]

MARTYN, FRANCIS, in Montserrat in 1677-1678. [TNA]

MARTYN, PATRICK, in the parish of Sandy Point, St Kitts on 7 February 1678. [TNA.COI. 42]

MARYMAN, THOMAS, in Montserrat in 1677-1678. [TNA]

MATALA, Sergeant DENNIS in Halfwaytree Division, St Kitts on 7 February 1678. [TNA.COI. 42]

MAUGHER, DANIEL, in Montserrat in 1677-1678. [TNA]

MAW, Sergeant WILLIAM, in St Thomas, Middle Island, St Kitts on 7 February 1678. [TNA.COI.42]

MAXWELL, JOHN, from Carrickfergus, emigrated to Philadelphia, Pennsylvania, in 1771. [BNL:19.3.1771]

MAYEN, JAMES, died in Donegal, Chester County, Pennsylvania, in 1734. [Lancaster County Historical Society, box 92, folder 1]

MAYNES, JAMES, a founder member of the Irish Charitable Society of Boston, Pennsylvania, in 1736. [UJA.II.1.18]

MAYNOR, REDMOND, in Montserrat in 1677-1678. [TNA]

MEAD, Sergeant DOMINICK, in Montserrat in 1677-1678. [TNA]

MEAGH, JOHN, in Montserrat in 1677-1678. [TNA]

MEAGHER, General THOMAS FRANCIS, born in Waterford on 3 August 1823, Governor of Montana, died 1 July 1867 in Fort Benton, USA. [GM.ns3/2.397]

MEAHAN, JOHN C., St Joseph's College, Memrancook, New Brunswick, son of James and Bridget Meahan in Ireland, a letter, 1877. [PANB.MC3075]

MEAKIN, ELIZABETH, born 1688, a spinster from Dublin, emigrated via Liverpool to America in 1704. [LRO]

MEANY, BRYAN, a surgeon from Waterford, died in Jamaica in 1795. [GMns65.616]

MEGH, WILLIAM, in Montserrat in 1677-1678. [TNA]

MERENANE, DANIEL, in Montserrat in 1677-1678. [TNA]

MEWARD, CORNELIUS, in Montserrat in 1677-1678. [TNA]

MIDDLETON, ROBERT, died 1732 in Chester County, Pennsylvania. [Lancaster County Historical Society, inventory box 92, folder 2]

MILLER, JOHN, formerly in Tobago, British West Indies, will, 1797. [PWI]

MILSON, WILLIAM, in Montserrat in 1677-1678. [TNA]

MISSETT, GARRETT, in Montserrat in 1677-1678. [TNA]

MITCHELL, ALEXANDER, emigrated from Ulster to Pennsylvania in 1719.

MITCHELL, WILLIAM, born 1 July 1689 in Londonderry, a Revenue Officer in America, a Loyalist, died 1804, buried in St Andrew's, Dublin. [GM.74.596]

MITCHELL, Captain, from Galway, died at Aux Cayes, St Domingo, in 1819. [GM.89.476]

MOLLY, JOHN, in Montserrat in 1677-1678. [TNA]

MONAGAN, PATRICK, cooper or sawyer from County Meath, emigrated via Liverpool to Quebec in 1827. [Montreal Gazette: 13.9.1830]

MONAGHAN, THOMAS, in Lower Canada, 1827. [NRS.GD45.3.534.8]

MONTGOMERY, GEORGE, born 1816, son of George Montgomery a merchant in Belfast, died in Barbados on 13 October 1839. [St Michael's Cathedral gravestone, Barbados]

MONTGOMERY, WILLIAM, in New York, will, 1782. [PWI]

MONTGOMERY, ..., emigrated from Londonderry aboard the Ardent bound for Baltimore, Maryland, in 1803. [NEHGR.LX.163]

MOORE, DAVID, in New Jerusalem, Queen's County, New Brunswick, a letter to brother Thomas Moore in County Donegal, 1840. He was born in 1801 and emigrated to New Brunswick with his wife Nancy Campbell and their son John in 1826. [PANB]

MOOR, SAMUEL, a founder member of the Irish Charitable Society of Boston, Massachusetts, in 1736. [UJA.II.1.18]

MOOR, THOMAS, from Dublin, an indentured servant bound from Liverpool to America in 1698. [LRO]

MOOR, WILLIAM, from Antrim, an indentured servant bound from Liverpool for America in January 1698. [LRO]

MORE, ROBERT, in Montserrat in 1677-1678. [TNA]

MORE, WILLIAM, in Montserrat in 1677-1678. [TNA]

MOREANE, JOHN, in Montserrat in 1677-1678. [TNA]

MOROONY, DANIEL, a court witness in St John's, Newfoundland, in 1789. [TNA.CO194.13.55]

MORRIS, ARTHUR, born 1739 in Ireland, a mariner and indentured servant, from London aboard the Maryland Planter bound for Maryland in 1775. [TNA.T47.9/11]

MORRIS, JAMES, in Montserrat in 1677-1678. [TNA]

MORRIS, NICHOLAS, in Montserrat in 1677-1678. [TNA]

MORRIS, THOMAS, son of Nathan Morris in Dublin, a cordiner, an indentured servant bond from Bristol to Barbados in January 1655. [BRO]

MORROUGH, NICHOLAS, born 1754, a dyer and lace weaver in Cork, via London aboard the Fortune bound for Maryland as an indentured servant in 1775. [TNA.T47.9/11]

MORTIMER, PHILIP, a founder member of the Irish Charitable Society of Boston, Massachusetts, in 1736. [UJA.II.1.18]

MORTOGH, DANIEL, in Montserrat in 1677-1678. [TNA]

MORTON, SAMUEL and JOHN, merchants in Philadelphia, Pennsylvania, a letter, 1769. [PRONI.D1044.176]

MULCLOKEY, JOHN, in Montserrat in 1677-1678. [TNA]

MULCLOKEY, PATRICK, in Montserrat in 1677-1678. [TNA]

MULGRAVE, WILLIAM, in Montserrat in 1677-1678.
[TNA]

MULKERE, KENNEDY, in Montserrat in 1677-1678.
[TNA]

MULLANE, JOHN, in Montserrat in 1677-1678. [TNA]

MULLAN, WILLIAM, in Montserrat in 1677-1678.
[TNA]

MULLOWNEY, JAMES, a merchant from Waterford, settled in Harbour Grace, Newfoundland, in 1765. [W.383]

MULRAGNE, DERMOND, in Montserrat in 1677-1678.
[TNA]

MULREAN, TEIGE, in Montserrat in 1677-1678. [TNA]

MULLREAN, THOMAS, in Montserrat in 1677-1678.
[TNA]

MULSTEROCK, MENOUS, in Montserrat in 1677-1678.
[TNA]

MUNNS, JAMES, emigrated from Sligo on 25 April 1847 aboard the Aeolus of Greenock bound for New Brunswick, landed at St John on 31 May 1847.
[PANB.MC803]

MURFEY, JOHN, in St Thomas, Middle Island, St Kitts on 7 February 1678. [TNA.COI.42]

MURPHY, ARTHUR, in Montserrat in 1677-1678. [TNA]

MURPHY, BRYAN, in Montserrat in 1677-1678. [TNA]

MURPHY, CORNELIUS, in Montserrat in 1677-1678.
[TNA]

MURPHY, CORNELIUS, in the parish of St John Capistar, St Kitts, on 28 January 1678. [TNA.COI.42]

MURPHY, DANIEL, in Montserrat in 1677-1678. [TNA]

MURPHY, DANIEL, son of Michael Murphy in Ballymure, County Tipperary, emigrated to USA in 1849, settled in New York and Illinois. [CA.CCCA.U76]

MURPHY, DAVID in St Thomas, Middle Island, St Kitts on 7 February 1678. [TNA.COI.42]

MURPHY, DENNIS, in Montserrat in 1677-1678. [TNA]

MURPHY, DERMOND, in the parish of Sandy Point, St Kitts on 7 February 1678. [TNA.COI.42]

MURPHY, DERMOND, in Montserrat in 1677-1678. [TNA]

MURPHY, EDMOND, in Montserrat in 1677-1678. [TNA]

MURPHY, EDWARD, in Montserrat in 1677-1678. [TNA]

MURPHY, EDWARD CREAGH, a planter in St Jan, Danish West Indies, died 20 July 1818, probate, St Jan, 1807-1826, fo.80/5]

MURPHY, JOHN, in Montserrat in 1677-1678. [TNA]

MURPHEY, JOHN, born in Ireland around 1732, a joiner and a convict-indentured servant, absconded from Alexandria, Fairfax County, Virginia, in 1760. [VaGaz;August, 1760]

MURPHY, MICHAEL, born 1753, a clerk and indentured servant from Cork, bound from London aboard the Fortune for Maryland in 1775. [TNA.T47.9/11]

MURPHY, MICHAEL, son of Michael Murphy in Ballymure, County Tipperary, emigrated to USA in 1849, settled in New York and Illinois. [CA.CCCA.U76]

MURPHY, PATRICK, in the parish of St John Capistar, St Kitts, on 28 January 1678. [TNA.COl.42]

MURPHY, TEIGE, in the parish of Sandy Point, St Kitts on 7 February 1678. [TNA.COl.42]

MURPHY, TEIGE, in Montserrat in 1677-1678. [TNA]

MURPHY, WILLIAM, in the parish of Sandy Point, St Kitts on 7 February 1678. [TNA.COl.42]

MURPHY, WILLIAM, from Ireland, accused of murder of William Quinn at Fermuse, near St John's, Newfoundland, in 1752. [TNA.CO194.13.55]

MURRAINE, DESMOND, in Montserrat in 1677-1678. [TNA]

MURRANE, THOMAS, in Montserrat in 1677-1678. [TNA]

MURRAY, ADAM, a tenant farmer in Tullywhisker, Urney parish, County Tyrone, bound for America in 1769. [PRONI.D623.A39.107]

MURRAY, Dr HUGH, born 1741 in Ireland, died in Bethlem, Connecticut, on 28 August 1815. [GM.ns85.634]

MURRAY, JOSEPH, an attorney in New York, husband of Grace Cosby, 17……..

MURRELL, HUGH, postmaster of Newcastle, Miramachi, New Brunswick, by 1842. [PANB.MC1058]

NACTON, TEAGUE, born 1607, emigrated via London aboard the Alexander bound for Barbados in May 1635. [TNA.E157.20]

NARRETT, JAMES, in the parish of Sandy Point, St Kitts on 7 February 1678. [TNA.COl.42]

NASH, PATRICK, in Montserrat in 1677-1678. [TNA]

NAUGHTON, DENNIS, in Montserrat in 1677-1678. [TNA]

NEAL, DANIEL, a founder member of the Irish Charitable Society of Boston, Massachusetts, in 1736. [UJA.II.1.18]

NEALE, MURLOW, in Montserrat in 1677-1678. [TNA]

NEALE, PATRICK, in Montserrat in 1677-1678. [TNA]

NEVILLE, THOMAS J., youngest son of the late Brent Neville of Ashbrooke, County Dublin, married Amelia Ransom, eldest daughter of Leander Ransom of New York, in Dublin on 16 December 1853. [GM.ns.41.309]

NEWCOMB, JOHN, in Montserrat in 1677-1678. [TNA]

NEWCOMB, ROBERT, in Montserrat in 1677-1678. [TNA]

NEWLAS, CORNELIUS, and a lady, in Montserrat in 1677-1678. [TNA]

NIBLOCK, Dr JAMES, emigrated from Ireland in 1803, settled in Brunswick County, Virginia, was killed on 5 July 1810. [GM.80.491]

NIMANE, RICHARD, in Montserrat in 1677-1678. [TNA]

NOBLE, HELEN, from County Antrim, emigrated to Petrolia, Canada, in 1879, letter. [PRONI.TD1424.11]

NOBLE, JOHN, a founder member of the Irish Charitable Society of Boston, Massachusetts, in 1736. [UJA.II.1.18]

NOGLE, JAMES, a tory who surrendered, taken to Dublin, to be transported beyond the sea, 19 October 1669. [CSPI.1669]

NORTON, KATEY, born around 1738 in County Wicklow, to Pennsylvania as an indentured servant in 1762, absconded from Robert Fulton in Lancaster County, Pennsylvania, in July 1763. [PaGaz:July 1763]

NUGENT, OLIVER, in Dominica in 1772. [JCTP.79.8/9]

NUGENT, RICHARD, M.D., from Dublin, married Elvira Crichton Sedgwick, eldest daughter of Samuel Sedgwick, M.D., in Antigua, on 29 February 1848. [GM.ns.29.538]

O'BRYAN, BRYAN, in Montserrat in 1677-1678. [TNA]

O'BRYAN, DANIEL, a soldier stationed at Placentia, Newfoundland, in 1732. [TNA.CO194.24.109]

O'BRYAN, DANIEL, a soldier of the 2nd Battalion of the 84th Regiment, commanded by Major John Small, aboard the frigate Raleigh, Captain Gambier, from New York bound for Charleston, South Carolina, in 1780. [NRS.GD174.2405]

O'BRYEN, MORGAN, settled in St Kitts before 1642 as a planter, dispossesed by Clement Everatt and banished to Crab Island, a petition in 1661. [PCCol.1661.520]

O'BRIAN, WILLIAM, 2nd Earl of Inchiquin, son of Murrough O'Brian (1614-1674), Governor of Jamaica from 1690 until his death in 1692. Probate 1692, PCC. [TNA]

O'CONNOR, MALACHI, sr., a West Indian merchant of Dublin, with his brother Valentine joint owner of the Mount William plantation in St Vincent, married [2] Lydia, widow of Bryan Blake of Antigua and St Vincent, died at Bath in 1821. [Caribeanna.333.82]

O'CONNERY, BRYNE DUFF, a tory who surrendered, taken to Dublin, to be transported beyond the sea, 19 October 1669. [CSPI.1669]

O'CONNOR, JOHN, from Middleton, County Cork, died in Honduras on 8 April 1804. [GM.74.690]

O'CONNOR, THOMAS, in New Roscommon near Bath, Steuben County, died in New York on 9 February 1855. [GM.43.544]

O'DONELL, ARTHUR, born 1795 in Clonmore, County Tipperary, son of Michael O'Donell and his wife Mary O'Neil, settled in Shubenacadie, Halifax County, Nova Scotia, died in Maitland, Hants County, Nova Scotia, on 20 November 1898. [Maitland gravestone]

O'DONEL, JAMES, born in Knocklofty, County Tipperary, Prefect Apostolic in Newfoundland from 1784

O'DONEL, MICHAEL, born 1777 in Tullaghmelan, County Tipperaray, a priest educated and ordained in Quebec in 1801, a priest in Newfoundland, Bishop in Quebec 1796, died 1832

O'DONNELL, WILLIAM L., a barrister, eldest son of the late Nicholas O'Donnell in Dublin, died in Grenada on 2 November 1866. [GM.ns.3.3.115]

O'DONOGHUE, PATRICK, an Irish rebel, died in New York in 1854. [GM.41.445]

O'FEENEY, MICHAEL, on the Murray of Broughton estate in Donegal, emigrated to America in 1732. [PRONI.D2860.12.28]

O'HAGAN, HENRY, a tory who surrendered, taken to Dublin, to be transported beyond the sea, 19 October 1669. [CSPI.1669]

O'HANLON, LAGHLIN, a tory who surrendered, taken to Dublin, to be transported beyond the sea, 19 October 1669. [CSPI.1669]

O'HARA, HENRIETTA, sister of Charles W. O'Hara in County Sligo, wife of Colonel McKinstry of the 17th Regiment, died in Toronto on 8 February 1867. [GM.ns3/3.541]

O'HARRA, JOHN, in Lower Canada, 1827. [NRS.GD45.3.534.8]

O'HEANNY, SHANE, a tory who surrendered, taken to Dublin, to be transported beyond the sea, 19 October 1669. [CSPI.1669]

OKINS, JOHN, in Montserrat in 1677-1678. [TNA]

O'MALLEY, ANTHONY, in Wardsville, Canada West, a letter, 1854. [NLI.ms21681]

O'MALLEY, THOMAS, a British Army physician from 1801-1826, graduated MD at St Andrews University in 1816, Health Officer on St Kitts, British West Indies. [StAUR]

O'MOLMOGHERY, BRYNE, a tory who surrendered, taken to Dublin, to be transported beyond the sea, 19 October 1669. [CSPI.1669]

O'MULLIN, JOHN, born 1617, emigrated via London aboard the Assurance of London, master Isack Bromwell, to Virginia in July 1635. [TNA.E157.20]

O'NEILL, CONN, a tory who surrendered, taken to Dublin, to be transported beyond the sea, 19 October 1669. [CSPI.1669]

O'NEILL, TERENCE J., in Toronto, Ontario, a letter, 1844. [NLI.24311]

O'REILLY, DOWELL, born in 1795, son of Matthew O'Reilly of Knock Castle, Louth, the Attorney General of Jamaica, died in St Andrews, Kingston, Jamaica, on 13 September 1855. [GM.ns.24.651]

O'RORKE, FRANCIS, a tory who surrendered, taken to Dublin, to be transported beyond the sea, 19 October 1669. [CSPI.1669]

O'ROURKE, FRANCIS, a tory who surrendered, taken to Dublin, to be transported beyond the sea, 19 October 1669. [CSPI.1669]

O'SULLIVAN, Captain FLORENCE, raised a company of soldiers in Barbados to regain St Kitts but was captured and imprisoned by the French 'in the island of Tothus Santus, a petition 1668. [PCCol.1668.741]

O'SULLIVAN, DENNIS, from Cork, a teacher at York Point, Mill Street, St John, New Brunswick, a letter, 1845. [PANB]

ORMSBY, EDWARD, an Irish convict servant, absconded, possibly, from King George County in March 1737. [VaGaz.4.1737]

OSBORNE, ROGER, from Ballycrenan, County Cork, Governor of Montserrat in 1660s.

OSBORNE, RICHARD BOYSE, an engineer in Canada, USA, and Panama, a diary 1834-1836 re Upper Canada. [NLI.7888-9]

PAINTER, JAMES, from Dublin, an indentured servant bound from Bristol to Barbados in 1660. [BRO]

PALMER, JOHN, from Ireland, an indentured servant bound from Bristol to Virginia in 1660. [BRO]

PARKE, ROGER, born 1754, a clerk from Dublin, via Bristol aboard the Fortune bound for Maryland as an indentured servant in 1775. [TNA.T47.9/11]

PARKHILL, JANE, from Aghadowey, emigrated to America in 1833, settled in Delhi, Delaware County, New York.

PARLANE, PATRICK, in Montserrat in 1677-1678. [TNA]

PARNELL, JOHN, author of 'Journal of a Tour in the United States and Canada', 1834. [NLI.2036]

PATERSON JOHN, an indentured servant, emigrated via Londonderry aboard the Hart, master Samuel Gordon, bound for New York in 1718. [BNL.27.10.1718]

PATTON, GEORGE W., emigrated from Tandragee, Ireland, to Barbados in 1841, died 7 January 1842. [St Michael's Cathedral, Barbados]

PELAWNE, MAURICE, in St Thomas, Middle Island, St Kitts on 7 February 1678. [TNA.COl.42]

PELHAM, PETER, a founder member of the Irish Charitable Society of Boston, Massachusetts, in 1736. [UJA.II.1.18]

PENDERGAST, THOMAS, a Lieutenant, stationed at Placentia, Newfoundland, in 1732. [TNA.CO194.24.109]

PHALSEY, DANIEL, in Montserrat in 1677-1678. [TNA]

PHELAN, PATRICK, a priest at Harbour Grace, Newfoundland, from 1784 until his death in 1800.

PHELAN, PATRICK, in Jamaica, will, 1800. [PWI]

PHILIPS, WILLIAM, born 1654, from Cork, emigrated via Liverpool bound for America in 1702. [LRO]

PHIPPS, LUKE ROCHE, son of William Phipps in Cork, a landowner in St Vincent in 1777, a barrister, died in Bermuda on 25 December 1787. [Caribbeana,3.82]

PICKETT, ROBERT, in Montserrat in 1677-1678. [TNA]

PILLSON, JAMES, in New York, letters, 1764-1765. [NLI.Balfour Papers]

PIM, FREDERICK W., in Canada, a journal, 1864. [PROI]

PINCKING, Reverend Guy R., born 1811, youngest son of the late Reverend W Pincking in Carrickmacross, County Monaghan, died in Charleston, Mississippi, on 4 September 1841. [GM.ns.16.660]

PLUNKETT, EDWARD, born 1615, emigrated via London aboard the Alexander bound for Barbados in May 1635. [TNA.E157.20]

PLUNKETT, ROBERT, born 1617, emigrated via London aboard the Alexander bound for Barbados in May 1635. [TNA.E157.20]

PLUNKETT, THOMAS, born 1607, emigrated via London aboard the Alexander bound for Barbados in May 1635. [TNA.E157.20]

POOR, EDMOND, in Montserrat in 1677-1678. [TNA]

POOR, NICHOLAS, in Montserrat in 1677-1678. [TNA]

POOR, RICHARD, at English Harbour, Antigua, will, 1798. [PWI]

POORE, ROBERT, in Montserrat in 1677-1678. [TNA]

POOR, WILLIAM, at Placentia, Newfoundland, a petitioner, 1744. [TNA.CO194.24.298]

POWELL, HUGH, a blacksmith from Dublin, an indentured servant bound from Liverpool to America in 1698. [LRO]

POWER, RICHARD, a soldier stationed at Placentia, Newfoundland, in 1732. [TNA.CO194.24.109]

PRICE, GEORGE, born 1803, from Bennett's Bridge, County Kilkenny, died on Tulloch Estate, Jamaica, on 15 April 1848. [GM.ns.30.110]

PRIOR, JOHN, a wigmaker and barber from Armagh, an indentured servant bound via London for Jamaica in 1753. [CLRO.ASP.8]

PULLEN, Mrs, born 1666, died in Antigua, British West Indies, in 1766. [FDJ.4126]

PURSELL, MORRISH, in Montserrat in 1677-1678. [TNA]

PURSILL, TOBIAS, in Montserrat in 1677-1678. [TNA]

QUAN, MICHAEL, a soldier of the 2nd Battalion of the 84th Regiment, commanded by Major John Small, aboard the frigate Raleigh, Captain Gambier, from New York bound for Charleston, South Carolina, in 1780. [NRS.GD174.2405]

QUIGLY, TEIGE, in Montserrat in 1677-1678. [TNA]

QUINAGAN, DANIEL, in Montserrat in 1677-1678. [TNA]

QUINGAYNE, PHILLIP, in Montserrat in 1677-1678. [TNA]

RALIFFE, DERMOND, in Montserrat in 1677-1678. [TNA]

RAMSEY, ..., emigrated from Londonderry aboard the Ardent bound for Baltimore, Maryland, in 1803. [NEHGR.LX.163]

RANKIN, MOSES, in Philadelphia, master of the Hercules, will, 1772. [PWI]

RATHELL, JOSEPH, from Dublin, a merchant in New Berne, North Carolina, a Loyalist, moved to London by 1776. [TNA.AO13.123.73-90]

RATHWELL, JOHN, born 1731, a tailor from Dublin, and indentured servant bound via London to Philadelphia in August 1751. [CLRO.ASP.63]

RAYLY, MORGAN, in Kayon Division, St Kitts on 7 February 1678. [TNA.COl.42]

RAYLY, THURLOGH in Halfwaytree Division, St Kitts on 7 February 1678. [TNA.COl.42]

RAYNE, JOHN, in Montserrat in 1677-1678. [TNA]

RAYNE, LOUGHLAN, in Montserrat in 1677-1678. [TNA]

READY, HUGH, in Montserrat in 1677-1678. [TNA]

REALY, HUGH, in Montserrat in 1677-1678. [TNA]

REAN, TEIGE, in Montserrat in 1677-1678. [TNA]

REAN, WILLIAM, in Montserrat in 1677-1678. [TNA]

REARDEN, ROGER, in Montserrat in 1677-1678. [TNA]

REARY, MURTOGH, in Montserrat in 1677-1678. [TNA]

REELY, OWEN, in Montserrat in 1677-1678. [TNA]

REEVE, ATER, in Montserrat in 1677-1678. [TNA]

REGAN, JOHN, in Montserrat in 1677-1678. [TNA]

REGAN, MORGAN, in Montserrat in 1677-1678. [TNA]

REGAN, RANDOLL, in Montserrat in 1677-1678. [TNA]

REGAN, ROGER, born 1754, a cook from Dublin, via London aboard the Fortune bound for Maryland as an indentured servant in 1775. [TNA.T47.9/11]

RENNY, JOHN, in Montserrat in 1677-1678. [TNA]

RERFIGGS, DERMOND, in Montserrat in 1677-1678. [TNA]

RENED, EDMOND, in Montserrat in 1677-1678. [TNA]

RERUANE, LAURENCE, in Montserrat in 1677-1678. [TNA]

REYNE, TEIGE, in Montserrat in 1677-1678. [TNA]

REYNOLDS, DANIEL, a soldier stationed at Placentia, Newfoundland, in 1732. [TNA.CO194.24.109]

REYTON, JOHN, in Montserrat in 1677-1678. [TNA]

RHEA, Reverend JOSEPH, a Presbyterian minister of Fahan, County Donegal, with his wife Elizabeth, and their children Matthew, John, Margaret, William, Elizabeth, Joseph, and Samuel, emigrated via Londonderry aboard the brig George bound for Philadelphia in September 1769. [Familia.22.33-50]

RIADEN, WILLIAM, in Montserrat in 1677-1678. [TNA]

RICE, NICHOLAS, in Barbados, will, 1768. [PWI]

RICHARDS, EDWARD, Captain Lieutenant of the 55th Regiment in St Lucia, will, 1798. [PWI]

RIKY, JOHN, emigrated to America in 1774, a merchant in Wilmington, North Carolina, a Loyalist in 1776, later in Dublin. [TNA.AO 13.123.146-151]

RILLROY, JOHN, in Montserrat in 1677-1678. [TNA]

RILLROY, WILLIAM, in Montserrat in 1677-1678. [TNA]

RINGE, ROGER, in Montserrat in 1677-1678. [TNA]

RISON, THOMAS, in Montserrat in 1677-1678. [TNA]

RITCHEY, ..., emigrated from Londonderry aboard the Ardent bound for Baltimore, Maryland, in 1803. [NEHGR.LX.163]

RITTANE, DERMOND, in Montserrat in 1677-1678. [TNA]

RITTANE, THOMAS, in Montserrat in 1677-1678. [TNA]

ROACH, JOHN, at Placentia, Newfoundland, a petitioner, 1744. [TNA.CO194.24.298]

ROACH, THOMAS, born in County Cork, settled in New York as a shipmaster, married in Trinity Church in 1778, buried there in 1795.

ROACH, WILLIAM, in the parish of St John Capistar, St Kitts, on 28 January 1678. [TNA.COl.42]

ROBERTS, JAMES, born 1753, a cordwainer from Ireland, from London aboard the Maryland Planter bound for Maryland in 1775. [TNA.T47.9/11]

ROBERTSON, JOHN, in Caledonia Street, St John, New Brunswick, a letter, 1847, possibly from Sligo. [PANB.MC803]

ROBINSON, HENRY, emigrated via Londonderry aboard the snow Frodsham, master James Aspinall, bound for Philadelphia in 1735, sought in 1740. [PaGaz.5.6.1740]

ROBINSON, JOHN, died 1722 in Chester County, Pennsylvania. [Chester County probate 157]

ROBRYAN, DANIEL, in Montserrat in 1677-1678. [TNA]

ROCH, JAMES, in Montserrat in 1677-1678. [TNA]

ROCHE, PATRICK, a planter on Montserrat, died in 1764. [FDJ.3805][GM.33.518]

ROCH, ROWLAND, in Montserrat in 1677-1678. [TNA]

ROCHE, Captain THOMAS, in Montserrat in 1677-1678. [TNA]

ROCK, NICHOLAS, in Montserrat in 1677-1678. [TNA]

ROE, JOHN, a gentleman in Antigua, will, 1717. [PWI]

ROGERS, JOHN, in St Thomas, Middle Island, St Kitts on 7 February 1678. [TNA.COI.42]

ROSS, DAVID R., born 22 March 1797, in Rosstrevor, County Down, Lieutenant Governor of Tobago, died there on 27 July 1851. [GM.ns.36.542]

ROSS, THOMAS, a mariner in Kington, Jamaica, will, 1782. [PWI]

ROWAN, JOHN J, eldest son of Reverend R W Rowan in Ahogill, County Antrim, married Mary Wright, eldest daughter of Georg Wright, the Colonial Secretary of Prince Edward Island, in Charlottetown, PEI, on 5 November 1866. [GM.ns3.3.104]

ROYLE, EDMOND, with a woman and a child, in Montserrat in 1677-1678. [TNA]

RUSSELL, PETER, born 1733, educated in Cork and at Cambridge University, fought in the French and Indian War as an officer of the 14th Regiment of Foot, later he fought in the American Revolution, in 1780 he was Captain of the 64th Regiment in the Leeward Islands, then Judge of the Vice Admiralty Court in Charleston, South Carolina, from 1792 he was Receiver General in Canada, he died in 1809. [PRONI.Mic205.1]

RUSSEL, WILLIAM, from Kinsale, an indentured servant in Liverpool bound for Barbados or the West Indies in 1698. [LRO]

RYAN, JOHN, from Montserrat, graduated from Leiden University in the Netherlands on 11 December 1769. [UL]

RYAN, SIMON, a soldier stationed at Placentia, Newfoundland, in 1732. [TNA.CO194.24.109]

ST LAWRENCE, JOSEPH, a founder member of the Irish Charitable Society of Boston, Massachusetts, in 1736. [UJA.II.1.18]

ST LEGER, BARRY, in Canada, letters, 1775-1779. [NRS.GD174.386]

SAWYER, JOHN, in Montserrat in 1677-1678. [TNA]

SAWYER, RICHARD, in Montserrat in 1677-1678. [TNA]

SCALLAN, THOMAS, born in Churchtown, Ballymore, County Wexford, in 1763, a priest in Newfoundland, died 1830.

SCANLAN, PATRICK, in Montserrat in 1677-1678. [TNA]

SCOTT, JOHN, and family settled in Donegal, Pennsylvania, by 1727. [Minutes of the Provincial Council of Pennsylvania, Vol.3.266]

SCOTT, JOHN, a merchant in Philadelphia, a letter, 1755. [PRONI.D354.1030]

SELLIOTT, RICHARD, in Montserrat in 1677-1678. [TNA]

SENNITT, WILLIAM, in Montserrat in 1677-1678. [TNA]

SEY, GARRETT, in Montserrat in 1677-1678. [TNA]

SEYMOUR, EDWARD, possibly from County Roscommon, in St John, New Brunswick, a letter, 1879. [PANB.MC1013]

SHANLY, ELLEN, only child of the late James Shanly from Normangrove, County Meath, married Major Charles Courtenay Villiers of the 47th Regiment, in Montreal on 5 February 1863. [GM.ns2.14.515]

SHANLY, FRANCIS, of the Abbey, Queen's County, born 1820, emigrated to Middlesex County, Upper Canada, in 1836, a civil engineer, died 1882. [PRONI.Mic205,1]

SHANNON, MARIA JANE, daughter of the late W C Shannon in County Clare, married George W Garden from Jamaica, in London on 28 October 1846. [GM.ns27.193]

SHARPE, JOHN, sr., in Montserrat in 1677-1678. [TNA]

SHARPE, JOHN, jr., in Montserrat in 1677-1678. [TNA]

SHAW, ARCHIBALD, in Philadelphia, will, 1787. [PWI]

SHAW, DERMOND in St Thomas, Middle Island, St Kitts on 7 February 1678. [TNA.COI.42]

SHAW, HENRY THOMAS, born 1823, fourth son of Lee Shaw, and nephew of Sir Robert Shaw of Bushy Park, [GM.ns22.446]

SHAW, SAMUEL, a trader in Lancaster County, Pennsylvania, died 1743. [Lancaster County Will Book.A-1.79]

SHEA, CORNELIUS, in Montserrat in 1677-1678. [TNA]

SHEA, DANIEL, in Montserrat in 1677-1678. [TNA]

SHEA, JOHN, in Montserrat in 1677-1678. [TNA]

SHEA, JOHN, a soldier of the 2nd Battalion of the 84th Regiment, commanded by Major John Small, aboard the frigate Raleigh, Captain Gambier, from New York bound for Charleston, South Carolina, in 1780. [NRS.GD174.2405]

SHEA, JOHN AUGUSTUS, born 1800 in Cork, a poet who settled in America in 1830, died in New York on 16 August 1845. [GM.ns24.429]

SHEA, PATRICK, in Montserrat in 1677-1678. [TNA]

SHEE, JOHN, jr., in Montserrat in 1677-1678. [TNA]

SHEEHAN, CORNELIUS, in Montserrat in 1677-1678. [TNA]

SHEEHAN, JAMES, from County Kilkenny to Newfoundland in 1858, correspondence, 1858 – 1892. [NLI.MS24559]

SHEEHAN, TERRENCE, a soldier of the 2nd Battalion of the 84th Regiment, commanded by Major John Small, aboard the frigate Raleigh, Captain Gambier, from New York bound for Charleston, South Carolina, in 1780. [NRS.GD174.2405]

SHEHY, [?], CHARLES, from Dublin, an indentured servant bound from Liverpool to America in 1698. [LRO]

SHERIDAN, JOHN, in Montserrat in 1677-1678. [TNA]

SHERIDAN, OWEN, died 11 February 1806, probate, St Jan, 1797-1807, fo.77. [RAK]

SHERIFF, THOMAS, born 14 November 1780 in Aghanloo, County Londonderry, settled in Barbados in 1800, died 29 July 1846. [St Paul's, Barbados]

SHIELS, Major General JAMES, in USA, letters, 1858, 1873-1875. [NLI.Photostat.5329]

SHIPBOY, ROBERT, in New York, a letter, 1766. [PRONI.D530.22]

SHONIN, PATRICK, in Montserrat in 1677-1678. [TNA]

SHOWLAND, DANIEL, from Cork, an indentured servant, at Liverpool aboard the Anne and Sarah, master John Marshall, bound for America in 1698. [LRO]

SINCLAIR, JOHN, possibly from Draperstown, County Londonderry, settled in Healdsburg, California, a letter, 1883. [PRONI.D1497.1.2]

SINCKLER, MARIA JANE, wife of J W Sinckler MD, daughter of the late Captain Patterson of the Royal

Marines in Dublin, died in Barbados on 25 October 1855.
[GM.ns45.96]

SKERRETT, STEPHEN, in Montserrat in 1677-1678.
[TNA]

SLATRY, JOHN, in Montserrat in 1677-1678. [TNA]

SLATRY, WILLIAM, in Montserrat in 1677-1678. [TNA]

SMILEY, THOMAS, emigrated via Londonderry aboard the snow Frodsham, master James Aspinall, bound for Philadelphia in 1735, sought in 1740. [PaGaz.5.6.1740]

SMITH, DARBY, a soldier of the 2nd Battalion of the 84th Regiment, commanded by Major John Small, aboard the frigate Raleigh, Captain Gambier, from New York bound for Charleston, South Carolina, in 1780.
[NRS.GD174.2405]

SMITH, EDWARD, born 1740, a laborer from Waterford, an indentured servant via London aboard the Peggy bound for Maryland in 1774. [TNA.T47.9/11]

SMITH, JOHN, in Montserrat in 1677-1678. [TNA]

SMITH, MARY ANN, in New Bandon, Gloucester, New Brunswick, a letter, 1857, daughter of William Sargent.
[PANB.MC1013]

SMITH, PHILIP, in America, letters, 1852-1853.
[NLI.Photostat 3235]

SMITH, RICHARD, emigrated from Sligo on 25 April 1847 aboard the Aeolus of Greenock bound for New Brunswick, landed at St John on 31 May 1847.
[PANB.MC803]

SMITH, WILLIAM, jr., settled in New York by 1768, letter. [BNL:1 July 1768]

SNOW, WILLIAM, in New York, 1782, letters to his brother Robert Snow in Waterford, Ireland. [NLI.Mansfield Papers]

SOUTHERLAND, DAVID, from Kilkenny, an indentured servant bound via Bristol to the colonies in January 1658. [BRO]

SOUTHWELL, Reverend HENRY GEORGE, of Trinity College, Dublin, died in Barbados on 25 February 1854. [GM.ns41.552]

SPAN, THOMAS, Captain in H.M.Army in New York, wills, 1763/1768. [PWI]

STAFFORD, FREDERICK, born 1822, seventh son of Brabazon Stafford in Dublin, died in Port of Spain, Trinidad, on 5 November 1857. [GM.ns2/4.112]

STARR, CHARLES E., from Roscrea, County Tipperary, of the US Army, letter, 1878. [NLI.Autograph Collection]

STATE, WILLIAM, in the parish of Sandy Point, St Kitts on 7 February 1678. [TNA.COI.42]

STEELE, Mrs, daughter of the late Robert Steele of Prospect Lota in County Cork, married George Hyde in St Vincent, on 7 October 1820. [GM.90.562]

STEPHENSON, JOHN, in the parish of Sandy Point, St Kitts on 7 February 1678. [TNA.COI.42]

STEWART, WILLIAM, a founder member of the Irish Charitable Society of Boston in 1736. [UJA.II.1.18]

SULLIVAN, CORNELIUS, in the parish of Sandy Point, St Kitts on 7 February 1678. [TNA.COI.42]

SULLIVAN, DANIEL in St Thomas, Middle Island, St Kitts on 7 February 1678. [TNA.COI.42]

SULLIVAN, Ensign DANIEL, on Montserrat in 1677-1678. [TNA]

SULLIVAN, DANIEL, in Montserrat in 1677-1678. [TNA]

SULLIVAN, DANIEL, in Montserrat in 1677-1678. [TNA]

SULLIVAN, DENNIS, in Montserrat in 1677-1678. [TNA]

SULLIVAN, DERMOND, in Montserrat in 1677-1678. [TNA]

SULLIVAN, FRANCIS, in Montserrat in 1677-1678. [TNA]

SULLIVAN, HUMPHREY, in Montserrat in 1677-1678. [TNA]

SULLIVAN, JOHN, in Montserrat in 1677-1678. [TNA]

SULLIVAN, MURTOW, in St Thomas, Middle Island, St Kitts on 7 February 1678. [TNA.COI.42]

SULLIVAN, OWEN, in Montserrat in 1677-1678. [TNA]

SULLIVAN, OWEN, a soldier stationed at Placentia, Newfoundland, in 1732. [TNA.CO194.24.109]

SULLIVAN, PHILIP, in Montserrat in 1677-1678. [TNA]

SULLIVAN, ROBERT, in Montserrat in 1677-1678. [TNA]

SULLIVAN, TEIGE, in Montserrat in 1677-1678. [TNA]

SULLIVAN, Sergeant TEAGE in Halfwaytree Division, St Kitts on 7 February 1678. [TNA.COI.42]

SULLIVAN, TEIGE DUF, in Montserrat in 1677-1678. [TNA]

SULLIVAN, THOMAS, a soldier stationed at Placentia, Newfoundland, in 1732. [TNA.CO194.24.109]

SWINEY, EDMUND, in Montserrat in 1677-1678. [TNA]

SWINEY, JOHN, in Montserrat in 1677-1678. [TNA]

SWINEY, MATTHEW, in Montserrat in 1677-1678. [TNA]

SWINEY, MICHAEL, in St Thomas, Middle Island, St Kitts on 7 February 1678. [TNA.COI.42]

SWINEY, NEALE, in Montserrat in 1677-1678. [TNA]

SWINEY, OWEN, in Montserrat in 1677-1678. [TNA]

SWINEY, WILLIAM, in Montserrat in 1677-1678. [TNA]

SYMONDS, ROBERT, in the parish of Sandy Point, St Kitts on 7 February 1678. [TNA.COI.42]

SYMMERS, ALEXANDER, in Montreal, son and heir of his father George Symmers, an attorney in Dublin, later in Galway, who died in December 1839. [NRS.S/H.1863]

TANNER, ELIZABETH, born in America, in Cork, will, 1805. [PWI]

TEIGE, DENNIS, in Montserrat in 1677-1678. [TNA]

TERRY, EDMOND, in Montserrat in 1677-1678. [TNA]

THEGHANE, DANIELL, in the parish of Sandy Point, St Kitts on 7 February 1678. [TNA.COI.42]

THEGHANE, DENNIS, in the parish of Sandy Point, St Kitts on 7 February 1678. [TNA.COI.42]

THEGHAN, TEAGE, in the parish of Sandy Point, St Kitts on 7 February 1678. [TNA.COI.42]

THOGAN, TIMOTHY, in St Thomas, Middle Island, St Kitts on 7 February 1678. [TNA.COI.42]

THOILL, JOHN, in Montserrat in 1677-1678. [TNA]

THOMAS, ARCHIBALD, a founder member of the Irish Charitable Society of Boston in 1736. [UJA.II.1.18]

THOMAS, JOHN, in Carolina, will, 1740. [PWI]

THOMAS, RICHARD, born 1681, from Dublin, aboard the Virginia Merchant, master Edmund Ball, bound from Liverpool to New England in March 1699. [LRO]

THOMPSON, JOHN, from Coleraine, aboard the Submission of Liverpool, master Thomas Seacombe, bound for Virginia in 1698. [LRO]

THOMPSON, JOHN, from Articlave, County Londonderry, a private of the 1st US Artillery, at Fort Sumter, South Carolina, in 1861, later in Fort Hamilton, New York, letters 1861. [PRONI.T1585]

THOMSON, RALPH, in St Thomas, Middle Island, St Kitts on 7 February 1678. [TNA.COI.42]

THOMPSON, SAMUEL, a planter on St Croix, will, 1795. [PWI]

THOMPSON, WILLIAM, born in Ireland emigrated to America in 1764, a maker of spinning wheels in St George's parish, Georgia, a Loyalist, moved to St Augustine, from there via Antigua to London by 1785, a Loyalist Claim. [TNA.AO12.101.246, etc.]

IRISH EMIGRANTS IN NORTH AMERICA, Volume 9

TOBEY, RICHARD, in the parish of St John Capistar, St Kitts, on 28 January 1678. [TNA.COI.42]

TOOL, ANN, born 1681, a spinster from Fingall, an indentured servant who emigrated via Liverpool aboard the Tabitha and Priscilla bound for America in 1702. [LRO]

TORRANS, JOHN, was born in County Londonderry in 1702, a merchant in New York, settled in South Carolina in 1758.

TRACY, EDMOND, in Montserrat in 1677-1678. [TNA]

TRACEY, JOHN, in Montserrat in 1677-1678. [TNA]

TRACY, MERMUSH, in Montserrat in 1677-1678. [TNA]

TRANT, DOMINICK, of Dingle, in Montserrat by 1724, died 1762. [Caribeanna.3.68]

TRANT, GARRETT, in Montserrat in 1677-1678. [TNA]

TULLY, HILLARY, in Carolina, will, 1740. [PWI]

TYLLYER, ..., in Antigua, will, 1663. [PWI]

VAUGHANE, DERMOND, in the parish of Sandy Point, St Kitts on 7 February 1678. [TNA.COI.42]

VAUGHAN, JOHN, formerly a Captain of the 17th Regiment of Foot, late from America, died in Portarlington, Ireland, in January 1763. [FDJ.3725]

VAUGHAN, LOGHLANE, in the parish of Sandy Point, St Kitts on 7 February 1678. [TNA.COI.42]

VERDEN, HUGH, in the parish of Sandy Point, St Kitts on 7 February 1678. [TNA.COI.42]

VINACK, JOHN, in the parish of Sandy Point, St Kitts on 7 February 1678. [TNA.COI.42]

WALKER, PATRICK, a founder member of the Irish Charitable Society of Boston in 1736. [UJA.II.1.18]

WALL, PATRICK, a soldier of the 2nd Battalion of the 84th Regiment, commanded by Major John Small, aboard the frigate Raleigh, Captain Gambier, from New York bound for Charleston, South Carolina, in 1780. [NRS.GD174.2405]

WALL, WILLIAM, a soldier stationed at Placentia, Newfoundland, in 1732. [TNA.CO194.24.109]

WALLACE, HUGH, formerly a merchant and councillor in New York, died in Waterford in 1788. [GM.58.178]

WALLACE, Captain NATHANIEL, and his wife Ann, emigrated from Sligo and settled in Woodbridge, Ontario, before 1844. [PRONI.Mic205/1]

WALSH, NATHANIEL, a founder member of the Irish Charitable Society of Boston in 1736. [UJA.II.1.18]

WALSH, THOMAS, a court witness in St John's, Newfoundland, in 1789. [TNA.CO194.13.55]

WARD, ELISHA, in St Thomas, Middle Island, St Kitts on 7 February 1678. [TNA.COI.42]

WARD, JAMES, son of Bryan Ward in Comer, Claudy, Ireland, emigrated to St John, New Brunswick, a letter, 1834. [PRONI]

WARD, JOHN, in Montserrat in 1677-1678. [TNA]

IRISH EMIGRANTS IN NORTH AMERICA, Volume 9

WARING, FREDERICK, born 1858, son of Lucas Waring in Lisburn, died in New York on 4 December 1888. [Blaris gravestone, County Down]

WARING, MARGARET, from Queen's County, Ireland, an indentured servant aboard the Elizabeth of Liverpool, bound for Virginia in 1699. [LRO]

WATTS, JAMES, from Ramelton, County Donegal, a merchant in Jamaica, letters 1800-1840. [PRONI.Mf135]

WATTS, SAMUEL, from Ramelton, County Donegal, a merchant in Barbados, letters 1800-1840. [PRONI.Mf135]

WEIR, WILLIAM, emigrated via Londonderry aboard the Provincialist to Pennsylvania, landed in Philadelphia on 6 August 1740. [PRONI.T1873.2]

WELCH, EDMOND, in Montserrat in 1677-1678. [TNA]

WELCH, MORRIS, in Montserrat in 1677-1678. [TNA]

WELCH, PATRICK, in Montserrat in 1677-1678. [TNA]

WELD, WILLIAM, in Montserrat in 1677-1678. [TNA]

WELSH, HONORA, born 1738 in Newfoundland, baptised in St Patrick's, Waterford on 7 December 1760.

WELCH, ULLICK, in Montserrat in 1677-1678. [TNA]

WESTOPHER, JOHN, in Montserrat in 1677-1678. [TNA]

WESTOPHER, THOMAS, in Montserrat in 1677-1678. [TNA]

WHELAN, JOHN, emigrated to Philadelphia, settled in Kensington, Pennsylvania, a letter, 1854. [PANB.MC2618; ms1.1.01]

WHITE, ELLINOR, in Barbados, will, 1738. [PWI]

WHITE, JAMES, in Montserrat in 1677-1678. [TNA]

WHITE, LAWRENCE, in the parish of Sandy Point, St Kitts on 7 February 1678. [TNA.COl.42]

WHITE, PATRICK, in Montserrat in 1677-1678. [TNA]

WHITE, STEPHENSON, from Belfast, died in Baltimore, Maryland, in February 1826. [GM.96.287]

WHITE, THOMAS in St Thomas, Middle Island, St Kitts on 7 February 1678. [TNA.COl.42]

WHITE, TURNS, born 1751, a farmer from Dublin, via London aboard the Baltimore bound for Baltimore as a redemptioner in 1775. [TNA.T47.9/11]

WILLIAMS, JOHN, in Montserrat in 1677-1678. [TNA]

WILLIAMS, TEAGE, an Irishman, a husbandman aged 18 years, emigrated aboard the Margaret bound for St Kitts in 1633. [TNA]

WILLICKS, ROGER, sr., in Montserrat in 1677-1678. [TNA]

WILLIACKS, ROGER, sr., in Montserrat in 1677-1678. [TNA]

WILSON, ROBERT, a merchant in Belfast, co-owner of the snow Arthur and Ann bound for Charleston, South Carolina in 1718. Charter party for the Hanover of Belfast in 1717, also one for the Friendship of Belfast in 1718. [PRONI.D354.363/369][TNA.CO5.508.71]

WOLFENDEN, JOHN, and family, from Lambeg, emigrated to Philadelphia in 1767. [BNL:20.2.1767]

IRISH EMIGRANTS IN NORTH AMERICA, Volume 9

WOODMAN, MATHEW, sr. and jr. in Montserrat in 1677-1678. [TNA]

WOODSIDE, Reverend JAMES, emigrated from Londonderry to New England in 1718. [Minutes of the Sub-Synod of Derry, 5 May 1718, number.50]

WORK, JOSEPH, a tanner in Pennsylvania, died in 1730s. [Lancaster County Historical Society, inventories, box 146, folder 6]

WYKE, JOHN, in Montserrat in 1677-1678. [TNA]

YOUNG, DAVID, born 1682 in Donegal, died 1776. [Worcester gravestone, New England]

YOUNG, JOHN, born in Londonderry in1623, died 1730. [Worcester gravestone, New England]

ZOUCH, AUGUSTA MARY ANNE, youngest daughter of the late Richard Zouch in Dublin Castle, married Reverend Charles Morice, in Quebec on 13 March 1845. [GM.ns24.72]

www.ingramcontent.com/pod-product-compliance
Lightning Source LLC
Chambersburg PA
CBHW071626170426
43195CB00038B/2139